engage

Level 2

Student Book

Gregory J. Manin   Alicia Artusi

OXFORD
UNIVERSITY PRESS

Contents

		Grammar	Vocabulary

Remember

Numbers 100–1000

1 Write the numbers.

112   239
734
650   677
332
591   1000

1 _one-hundred twelve_
2 _____
3 _____
4 _____
5 _____
6 _____
7 _____
8 _____

2 🎧 Listen. Circle the number you hear.
1 116 / (160)
2 430 / 413
3 856 / 866
4 223 / 203
5 119 / 190

Dates

1 Write the dates.
1 06/21 _June twenty-first_
2 08/11 _____
3 09/02 _____
4 04/30 _____
5 12/07 _____

2 When's your birthday? _____

Feelings

1 Fill in the blanks with the words below.

> happy   angry   tired   scared   surprised   nervous

1 I'm very __happy__ because I passed my exam!
2 Lily was _____ when she saw a blue banana.
3 We're _____. We have an exam tomorrow.
4 My mom gets _____ when I come home late.
5 They're _____ because they're climbing a mountain.
6 Ben was _____ when he saw a tiger in his garden.

Food

1 Fill in the blanks in the menu with the words below.

> muffins   soda   apples   cheese   milk   yogurts   chicken

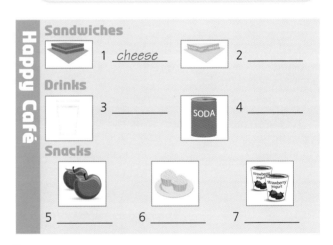

Happy Café

Sandwiches
1 _cheese_   2 _____

Drinks
3 _____   4 _____

Snacks
5 _____   6 _____   7 _____

2 Fill in the blanks with *some* or *any*.
1 There are __some__ cheese sandwiches.
2 There aren't _____ ham sandwiches.
3 There is _____ milk.
4 There isn't _____ orange juice.
5 There are _____ muffins.
6 There isn't _____ diet soda.

Object pronouns

1 Fill in the chart with the correct pronouns.

Personal pronoun	Object pronoun
I	1 _me_
you	2 ____
3 ____	him
she	4 ____
5 ____	it
we	6 ____
7 ____	you
they	8 ____

2 Fill in the blanks with the words below.

> us   him   her   me   them

Give it to (1) _her_.

Don't give it to (2) ____!
Give it to (3) ____.

Don't give it to (4) ____.
Give it to (5) ____!

Clothes

1 Matt is going on summer vacation to stay with his friend, Katie. Fill in the blanks in Katie's letter.

Hi Matt
It's hot and sunny right now, so you need summer clothes. But we can go skiing in summer, too, so you also need winter clothes!

For hot weather:
1 ____ sneakers ____
2 _____
3 _____
4 _____
5 _____

For skiing:
6 _____
7 _____
8 _____
9 _____
10 _____

See you on Saturday!
Katie

Parts of the body

1 Write the clothes from the exercise above next to the parts of the body.

HEAD	1	_cap_	2	_____
EYES	3	_____		
BODY	4	_____	5	_____
	6	_____	7	_____
HANDS	8	_____		
FEET	9	_____	10	_____

Adjectives (objects)

1 Look at Matt's suitcase. Fill in the blanks with the adjectives below.

> small   soft   thick   heavy   long
> expensive   old

Matt is taking his (1) _____old_____ sneakers on
vacation with him. He's also taking an
(2) _____ camera, and (3) _____ skis.
In his suitcase there is a (4) _____ book about
Canada, and a (5) _____ towel for swimming.
His suitcase is _____!

2 Write the opposites of the adjectives.

1 old _new_____
2 soft _____
3 heavy _____
4 long _____
5 expensive _____

Invitations

1 Katie is inviting her friends to go to a music
festival. Fill in the blanks with the phrases
below.

> I'm sorry   Sure   Let's   Would you like to

Katie: (1) __Would you like to__ go to the
music festival?

Matt: (2) _____.

Katie: (3) _____ go to the music festival!

Ricardo: (4) _____, I can't. I have to study.

Appearance

1 Look at the picture of Katie and her friends.
Write the correct name(s) next to the sentences.

1 She has brown eyes. _Anita_
2 She isn't wearing sneakers. _____
3 She has wavy hair. _____
4 They're wearing green sneakers. _____ and

   _____
5 He doesn't have curly hair. _____
6 He doesn't have brown eyes. _____
7 They have blond hair. _____ and _____
8 She's tall. _____

Present progressive

1 Fill in the blanks in the chart.

Affirmative	Negative
I (1) _am_ eating a burger.	I'm not eating a pizza.
He (2) _____ dancing.	He (3) _____ running.
We (4) _____ studying.	We (5) _____ watching TV.

2 Look at the picture on page 6. Write affirmative and negative sentences. Use the present progressive.

1 Katie / dance / sing
   Katie is dancing _____.
   She isn't singing _____.

2 Lucio / eat a burger / eat French fries
   _____.
   _____.

3 Matt / laugh / shout
   _____.
   _____.

4 Anita / drink milk / drink a soda
   _____.
   _____.

3 Fill in the blanks in the chart.

Yes / no questions	Answers
(1) _Are_ they drinking soda?	Yes, they (2) _____ . / No, they (3) _____ .
(4) _____ she having lunch?	Yes, she is. / No, she (5) _____ .

wh- questions	Answers
What (6) _____ you doing?	I'm writing a letter.
Where (7) _____ he going?	He's going to the beach.

4 Put the words in order to make questions. Write the answers.

1 is / Katie / a red T-shirt / wearing?
   Is Katie wearing a red shirt? _Yes, she is_ .

2 Anita / dancing / is?
   _____? _____.

3 are / Lucio and Matt / blue sneakers / wearing?
   _____? _____.

4 drinking / Anita / what / is?
   _____? _____.

5 Lucio / is / eating a burger?
   _____? _____.

Simple present

1 Fill in the blanks in the chart.

Affirmative	Negative
We have breakfast at 7 a.m.	We (1) _don't_ get up early.
She watches TV in the evening.	She (2) _____ have lunch at school.

2 Matt is e-mailing his family. Fill in the blanks with the correct form of the simple present.

Hi guys,

I'm in a cyber café with Lucio right now. We are having a great time in Toronto with Katie.

Katie (1) _lives_ (live) 3km from the city centre in big house.

My life during the week in very quiet. I (2) _____ (get up) early every morning. Katie and I (3) _____ (have) breakfast with her dad, and then he (4) _____ (drive) us to the city. There are so many things to do there.

We (5) _____ (go) to the museums, and the zoo too!

See you soon,
Matt

3 Make the sentences negative.

1 Katie lives 6 km from the city.
   Katie doesn't live 6 km from the city .

2 Matt and Katie go to the movies.
   They _____.

3 Katie and Matt have breakfast with Katie's brother.
   _____.

4 Katie's dad drives them to the beach.
   _____.

5 Matt gets up late.
   _____.

4 Fill in the chart.

yes / no questions	Answers
(1) _Do_ you go to school at 8 a.m.?	Yes, I do. / No, I (2) _____ .
(3) _____ he play soccer on the weekend?	Yes, he (4) _____ . / No, he doesn't.

wh- questions	Answers
When do they get up?	At 7 a.m.
Where (5) _____ she go on vacation?	She goes to the mountains.

5 Write the questions for Katie. Use the words in parentheses.

You: (1) _Where do you live Katie_ ?
(where / you / live)

Katie: I live in Toronto, in Canada.

You: Cool! And (2) _____ _____ ?
(where / Matt / live)

Katie: Matt lives in Glasgow, in Scotland.

You: (3) _____ ?
(what / you / do on the weekend)

Katie: On the weekend, I go to concerts and I play the drums.

You: Cool! (4) _____ ?
(what kind of music / you / like)

Katie: I like rock music.

You: Thanks, Katie.

Review it!

1 You need a dice. Work with a partner. Throw the dice (1–6) and answer the questions.

Describe a classmate. (hair, eyes, clothes).

Your partner guesses who it is.

How many parts of the body can you name?

Describe an object in the classroom . Use four adjectives.

Your partner guesses what it is.

How many food items can you name?

Mime / draw two feelings (tired, scared, ...).

Your partner guesses the word.

**Test your partner on dates.
You: twelve six (12/06)
Your partner:
December sixth**

1 Our world

Grammar: gerunds (-ing form); *much / many / a lot of*
Vocabulary: sports and hobbies; city life

ntroducing the topic

Vocabulary

1 Match the words with the photos. Write the correct number next to the words.

7	shopping	☐	playing soccer
☐	playing in a band	☐	acting
☐	working on a computer	☐	scuba diving
☐	painting	☐	running

🎧 **Now listen and repeat.**

Recycling

2 Make sentences about the activities with these adjectives.

Playing soccer is fun, but running is boring.

 exciting
fun
interesting
 OK
boring
 awful

9

Exploring the topic

FRIEND FINDER

Hi! My name is Anh Vu. I'm from Hanoi, Vietnam. I'm fifteen years old and I'm in high school. I love painting, and I enjoy reading. Swimming and scuba diving are fun, too. I hate running! Running is awful.

Hola! My name is Carlos Vargas. I'm fourteen years old and I live in Caracas, Venezuela. I'm in the eighth grade. I love playing soccer and basketball. Working on a computer is cool, too. Listening to music is OK. I don't like singing. My singing is terrible, and my friends laugh at me!

Hello. My name is Andreas Stavras. I'm sixteen years old and I live in Athens, Greece. I'm in high school. I love acting. Acting is fun. I like playing in my band, Generescence, too. I play the guitar. I don't like playing soccer or basketball, but playing tennis is OK. What about you?

Hey! My name is Liliana Serrano. I'm fifteen years old and I live in Rio de Janeiro, Brazil. I love water sports. Scuba diving is exciting! I like skateboarding, too. I enjoy listening to music. My favorite group is Moby. I hate shopping! It is SO boring!

Reading

1 Read the text quickly. Check (✓) the information that appears in the text.

1 name   _____
2 age   _____
3 family   _____
4 likes   _____
5 dislikes   _____
6 appearance _____

2 🎧 Read and listen to the text. Fill in the blanks with the names of the people.

1 _*Anh*_ doesn't like running.
2 _____ enjoys playing soccer.
3 _____ likes painting.
4 _____ loves acting.
5 _____ likes working on the computer.
6 _____ doesn't enjoy shopping.
7 _____ doesn't like singing.
8 _____ and _____ like scuba diving.

Grammar

Gerunds (-ing form)

Talking about personal tastes

1 Look at the chart.

like / enjoy / love / don't like / hate + -ing form		
I / You / We / They	**love**	sing**ing**.
He / She / It	**enjoys**	read**ing**.

2 Put 😊 or ☹ next to the sentences.

1   Kim doesn't like playing basketball. ☹
2   I enjoy reading and writing. __
3   They hate running. __
4   Susie loves shopping. __
5   Tom and Sammy like playing baseball. __
6   I don't like playing tennis. __

Take note!

Spelling rules for *-ing* forms
1 **Regular: add** *-ing*.
   read ➔ read**ing**
2 **One vowel + one consonant: double the consonant +** *-ing*.
   run ➔ ru**nn**ing
3 **Consonant +** *-e*: ~~e~~ + *-ing*.
   ride ➔ rid**ing**

3 Fill in the blanks with the *-ing* form of the correct verb.

ride   read   run   do   shop   play

1   John loves ____riding____ his bike.
2   I don't like _____ soccer.
3   We love _____. Buying new clothes is fun!
4   Carlos enjoys _____ books about science.
5   Evan and Tania like _____ in marathons.
6   Do you like _____ homework?

4 Look at the chart.

-ing form + be + adjective		
Running	**is**	awful.
Riding a bike	**is**	fun.

5 Look at the pictures. Write sentences.

2 paint / fun
1 play tennis / hard
3 skateboard / exciting
4 play in a band / cool
5 watch TV / boring
6 read / interesting

1   *Playing tennis is hard*   .
2   _____ .
3   _____ .
4   _____ .
5   _____ .
6   _____ .

Finished?
Page 105, Puzzle 1A

Over to you!

6 Write two true sentences and one false sentence using the verbs *love*, *like* and *hate*. Can the class guess the false sentence?

Student A: 1 I love reading.
              2 I like running.
              3 I hate listening to music.
Student B: Sentence 3 is false.
Student A: You're wrong. / You're right.

Building the topic

Vocabulary

1 Match the words with the photos. Write the correct letter next to the word.

- [6] litter
- [ ] noise
- [ ] traffic
- [ ] pollution
- [ ] houses
- [ ] open spaces
- [ ] tall buildings
- [ ] entertainment

🎧 Now listen and repeat.

2 🎧 Read and listen to the text. Write the number of the correct picture next to the sentences.

3 Write C (countable) or U (uncountable) next to the words.

1 pollution _U_
2 litter ____
3 tall buildings ____
4 noise ____
5 open spaces ____
6 entertainment ____
7 traffic ____
8 houses ____

WHERE WE LIVE

Like most big cities, there's a lot of pollution. But l love it here. It's really exciting. _1_

There are a lot of cars, trucks and buses, so there's a lot of noise! ____

There isn't much traffic in my village. There are only about fifty cars! ____

There are a lot of open spaces where l live. It's really nice. ____

There are a lot of tall buildings, and they are building more every day. ____

There are a lot of small houses, but we don't have tall buildings. ____

There isn't much litter in the streets. It's very clean. ____

There's a lot of entertainment. There are movie theaters, music clubs and cafés. It's great! ____

Grammar
much / many / a lot of

Talking about quantity

1 **Look at the chart.**

Countable	Uncountable
How many people are there?	**How much** noise is there?
There are **a lot of** people.	There's **a lot of** noise.
There are**n't many** people.	There is**n't much** noise.

2 **Circle the correct word(s).**

1 There are much / a lot of cars in my town.
2 How much / many people live in your city?
3 There's a lot of / much pollution in big cities.
4 There aren't many / much movie theaters in my town.
5 There's much / a lot of noise in our classroom.
6 There aren't many / much skaters in the skating rink.

3 **Look at the picture and fill in the blanks with *much*, *many*, or *a lot of*.**

1 There's _a lot of_ noise.
2 There aren't _____ trees.
3 There are _____ bicycles.
4 There aren't _____ cars.
5 There's _____ of entertainment.
6 There isn't _____ litter.

Finished?
Page 105, Puzzle 1B

4 **Write the questions. Use the answers to help you.**

1 _How many CDs do you have_ ?
   I have about 250 CDs.
2 _____?
   I do a lot of homework – about 4 hours a day.
3 _____?
   I have a lot of friends.
4 _____?
   There aren't many parks in my neighborhood.
5 _____?
   There isn't much noise in my house. We're pretty quiet.
6 _____ hours of TV do you watch?
   Only about an hour a day.

Over to you!

5 **Look at exercise 4 again. Ask and answer in class.**

Student A: How many CDs do you have?
Student B: I have about 20 CDs.
Student A: How much homework ... ?

Living English

MY TWO LIVES

by Nikos Tsomos

My family and I have two lives. In the winter, we live in Athens, Greece. In the summer, we live in the small village where my mother and father are from. It's on the island of Naxos. The two places are very different.

In Athens, we live in a tall building with twelve floors. Our apartment is big. It has six rooms and two balconies. In our village we live in a small house. It has one floor, and there aren't many rooms. There are a lot of trees around the house, and there aren't many other houses.

Athens has a lot of people. There are about ten million people in the city. That's about half the population of Greece! There aren't many people in our village – only about 200. I enjoy going out with other young people in Athens, but I don't have many friends in the village because there aren't many young people there.

There are a lot of things to do in the city. There are movie theaters, cafés and dance clubs. There are also places to play video games, and cyber cafés. I love watching sports. Athens has a lot of stadiums and sports fields. It's a fun, exciting place. It's different in the village. There are two restaurants and there's one movie theater. There aren't any cyber cafés. But there are open spaces, and there's a beach near the village too! I like going to the beach.

I feel very lucky because we live in two places. I love living in the big city, and I love staying in the village too. I think I have the best of both worlds.

Reading 🎧

Before you read

1 Look at the two pictures and the title of the article. Do you think Nikos lives:

  a in a village?
  b in a city?
  c in a village AND in a city?

While you read

2 Answer the questions.

  1 Write two things Nikos likes about the city.
  2 Write two things he likes about the village.

After you read

3 Look at the Reading skills box.

Reading skills

Key words

Key words are the most important words in an article. They tell you the main ideas, and they help you to answer questions.

Now read the article quickly. Find the key words for the following ideas in the article.

1 population and social life: *people, population, going out, young people, friends*
2 where people live: *tall building,* …
3 entertainment:

4 Read the article again. Fill in the blanks.

1 Nikos's family lives in the village in *the summer*.
2 Nikos's apartment in Athens is _____.
3 The population of Nikos's village is about _____.
4 In the village, Nikos doesn't have many _____.
5 Nikos loves _____ sports.
6 There aren't any _____ in the village.
7 There is a _____ near the village.

Listening 🎧

1 Listen to the dialog. What is Mike and Deb's favorite activity?

2 Listen to the dialog again. Fill in the blanks with the words below.

> entertainment   theater   quiet
> homework   club   acting   New York

1 Mike is from _New York_ .

2 For Mike, the town is really _____ .

3 There isn't much _____ in the town.

4 Deb goes to a tennis _____ .

5 Mike likes tennis and _____ .

6 There is a _____ group at the school.

7 They don't do much _____ at the school.

Writing

1 Read the postcard. Where is it from? Is the writer happy there?

> Hi Manuel!
> Greetings from Tucson. I like living here. It's a cool place. There are a lot of nice houses, and there are a lot of parks and open spaces. There isn't much pollution or litter. There are a lot of places to play soccer. I love going to the stadium and watching the games. I like going to school here, too. The other kids are great, and the teachers are nice.
> There are a few things I don't like. There aren't many cafés, so I meet my friends at the mall or a fast food restaurant. That's boring. Also, there aren't any beaches! But generally it's a great place.
>
> Best wishes,
> Anna

2 Read the postcard again. Underline the things Anna likes in red and the things Anna doesn't like in blue. Fill in the chart with the information from Anna's postcard.

Name of place	Tucson
She likes:	nice houses, green spaces, not much pollution or litter
She doesn't like:	

3 Now imagine you are living in a different place and make notes about your place.

4 Write a postcard about the place in exercise 3. Use the text and your notes to help you.

Review 1

Vocabulary
Sports and hobbies

1 Fill in the blanks with the phrases below.

> acting   playing soccer   painting
> playing in a band   working on a computer
> running   scuba diving   shopping

1 Julian loves _____ *playing soccer* _____ .
2 Carla thinks _____ is cool.
3 Melody enjoys _____ .
4 Ang doesn't like _____ .
5 Alessandro loves _____ .
6 Teresa thinks _____ is boring.
7 _____ is interesting.
8 For Kelly, _____ is really exciting.

City life

2 Match the nouns with the words below.

> pollution   noise   houses   entertainment
> traffic   tall buildings   open spaces   litter

1 offices or apartments = _*tall buildings*_
2 dirty air and water = _____
3 movies and live music = _____
4 trash in the street = _____
5 a lot of cars = _____
6 parks = _____
7 sounds of cars and planes = _____
8 places for people to live = _____

Grammar
Gerunds (-ing form)

1 Write sentences about Daniel Radcliffe's likes and dislikes.

1 enjoy / spend time with parents _He enjoys_
   spending time with his parents .
2 love / act _____
   _____
3 like / watch movies _____
   _____
4 not like / do homework _____
   _____
5 enjoy / help other people _____
6 love / listen to music _____
   _____

much / many / a lot of

2 Write questions and answers as in the example.
\+ = a lot of and – = not much.

1 noise – _How much noise is there_ ?
   There isn't much noise .
2 people + _____?
   _____.
3 pollution – _____?
   _____.
4 parks + _____?
   _____.
5 buildings + _____?
   _____.
6 entertainment – _____?
   _____.

Study skills

1 Using your coursebook

Engage has different types of material to help you study.

Look at this list. Where can you find these things?

1 "I want to know how many units are in the book." Page ___
2 "I want to find a list of the vocabulary in unit 1." Page ___
3 "I want to do a puzzle related to this unit." Page ___
4 "I want to study grammar explanations for unit 1." Page ___

Grammar: simple present and present progressive; *have to*
Vocabulary: activities; household chores

Introducing the topic

Vocabulary

1 Match the words with the rooms. Write the correct number 1–3 next to the words.

3 go to school	☐ eat fast food
☐ play an instrument	☐ play basketball
☐ listen to music	☐ go climbing
☐ watch movies	☐ read magazines

🎧 Now listen and repeat.

Recycling

2 Look at the verbs on the wheel. Write the time you do the activities.

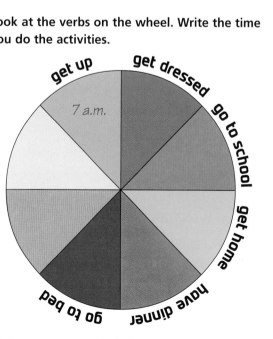

get up · get dressed · go to school · get home · have dinner · go to bed

7 a.m.

3 Add two more verbs and times to the wheel.

Exploring the topic

Two old school friends,
Nick and Tom, meet online.

| 1 | First name: Tom | Last Name: Lindon | Where do you live now? NY, USA. |
| 2 | First name: Nick | Last Name: Ridley | Where do you live now? Iceland. |

Tom: Hi Nick. I can't believe you're in Iceland. Where do you live exactly?

Nick: I live in a very small village called Sudavik. There are mountains, glaciers and beaches. It's quiet but fun. How's life in New York?

Tom: Cool. I'm on the school basketball team. I play with Matt. Do you remember him from elementary school?

Nick: Sure. Funny guy.

Tom: Matt is here in my house right now.

Nick: Really? What's he doing?

Tom: He's watching a soccer match downstairs. But tell me something about you. What do you usually do on the weekend?

Nick: I don't go out much. I usually meet my friends, make dinner and watch movies.

Tom: What do you eat in Iceland?

Nick: A lot of fish and pancakes. Right now my mom is making pancakes, and my sister Nadia is studying Icelandic. What about you? Do you go out a lot?

Tom: Yes. There's a lot of entertainment in New York. I usually go to the movies in the winter, and to concerts in the summer. Matt and I sometimes go to dance clubs on Saturdays.

Nick: Where are you now?

Tom: I'm in my bedroom. I'm listening to music on my computer.

Nick: Can you send me some photos of our school friends?

Tom: Sure, Nick. Let's keep in touch.

Reading

1 Read the text. Circle T (True) or F (False).

1 Tom and Nick are chatting online.   T / F
2 They are friends from elementary school.   T / F
3 Tom lives in New York.   T / F
4 Nick lives in a big city.   T / F
5 Matt is watching a soccer match right now.   T / F
6 Nick goes to dance clubs on the weekend.   T / F
7 Nick's sister is making pancakes right now.   T / F
8 Tom is listening to music on his computer.   T / F

2 🎧 Read and listen to the text. Match 1–5 with A–E.

1 Nick's sister Nadia   A is making pancakes right now.
2 Nick usually   B eat a lot of fish.
3 Nick's mom   C is studying Icelandic right now.
4 Icelandic people   D goes to the movies in the winter.
5 Tom   E meets his friends on the weekend.

Grammar

Simple present and present progressive

Talking about regular activities and things that are happening right now

1 Look at the chart.

Simple present	Present progressive
I watch TV **every evening**.	He's watching a soccer match **right now**.
She doesn't play tennis **on the weekend**.	They aren't playing basketball **right now**.
Do they have dinner **at six o'clock**?	Are you eating a burger **right now**?
When do you get up?	What is he doing **right now**?

2 Look at the pictures of Yoshi Zang, a clothes designer. Circle the correct answer.

Monday to Friday
Right now

1 (a) He usually designs clothes.
  b He's designing clothes right now.

2 a He usually listens to music.
  b He's listening to music right now.

3 a He usually works with other people in his studio.
  b He's talking to people right now.

4 a He usually shows his designs in his studio.
  b He's showing his new designs right now.

5 a He usually wears a suit.
  b He's wearing a suit right now.

3 Fill in the blanks with the correct tense. Use the simple present or present progressive.

Hi. I'm Yoshi from Japan. I'm a clothes designer.
I usually (1) _____work_____ (work) in my studio, but
right now I (2) _____ (design) some T-shirts in
my sister's apartment.
My sister Hana, always (3) _____ (help) me.
She usually (4) _____ (look) at my designs
and (5) _____ (make) some changes.
Right now she (6) _____(wear) a T-shirt with
one of my designs on it.
We usually (7) _____ (go) to fashion
exhibitions together and (8) _____ (meet)
other designers.

Finished?
Page 105, Puzzle 2A

Over to you!

4 What does your room say about you?

1 Write three things about you in this keyhole.
  You can use sport, hobbies, TV shows and music.

2 Tell the class.

3 The class makes sentences about you.

1 rap
2 basketball
3 Real Madrid

Student A: 1 rap, 2 basketball, 3 Real Madrid
Student B: You like listening to rap. You play basketball. Real Madrid is your favorite soccer team.

Building the topic

Vocabulary

1 Look at the pictures. Fill in the blanks with the words below.

> make (your) bed   clean (your) room
> set the table   put away   wash the dishes
> take out the garbage   cut the grass
> make lunch

🎧 Now listen and repeat.

2 Write the chore in the correct row.

bedroom	*make your bed*
kitchen	
dining room	
yard	

1 I have to _make_ my _bed_ .

2 I don't have to make my bed, but I have to _____ _____ _____. I hate it!

3 I have to _____ my _____, but my brother doesn't have to. It isn't fair!

4 My sister has to _____ _____ her clothes. She has a lot of clothes!

5 I have to _____ _____ _____. There are nine people in my family!

6 My brother has to _____ _____ _____ _____. It's smelly!

7 I have to _____ _____ for my little brother. He's always hungry!

8 My sister has to _____ _____ _____. It's hard work!

Grammar

have to

Talking about obligation

1 Look at the chart.

Obligation		No obligation	
I / You	**have to** set the table.	I / You	**don't have to** wash the dishes.
He / She / It	**has to** cut the grass.	He / She / It	**doesn't have to** make lunch.
You / We / They	**have to** wash the dishes.	You / We / They	**don't have to** set the table.

Questions	Short answers
Do you **have to** help in the house?	Yes, I do. / No, I don't.
Does he / she **have to** help in the house?	Yes, she does. / No, she doesn't.

2 Fill in the blanks with *have to* or *has to*.

1 My sister _has to_ put away her things.

2 My friends _____ cut the grass.

3 I _____ set the table on Sundays.

4 My brother _____ take out the garbage at weekends

5 My sister and I _____ make our beds every day.

3 Fill in the blanks with *have to / has to* (✓) or *don't have to / doesn't have to* (✗).

1 A doctor _has to_ wear a uniform. (✓)

2 A singer _____ wear a uniform. (✗)

3 Teachers _____ work with children. (✓)

4 Models _____ look fashionable all the time. (✗)

5 A flight attendant _____ speak all languages. (✗)

6 A mechanic _____ fix cars. (✓)

4 Look at the college rules. Write sentences.

College rules

1 Lock your room door.
You have to lock your room .

2 Turn off the lights after midnight.
_____ .

3 Come home before 11 p.m.
_____ .

4 Put away your things.
_____ .

Not necessary, but welcome ...

5 Cut the grass.
You don't have to cut the grass .

6 Clean your room.
_____ .

7 Take out the garbage.
_____ .

Finished?
Page 105, Puzzle 2B

Over to you!

5 Write 3 chores that you have to do.
Ask another student. Does s/he have to do the same household chore?

Student A: Do you have to make your bed?
Student B: Yes, I do. / No, I don't.

Living English

Unusual jobs

Are you looking for a summer job? Here are some unusual ideas!

A Nam is a "golf ball diver". What does he do? He looks for lost golf balls underwater. He usually finds about 5000 golf balls in one day! In the photo Nam is looking for a ball in a deep lake in his scuba diving suit. Nice job for the summer.

B Look at this woman. Her name is Maria. She's an "odor judge". She smells all kinds of things: cat food, diapers, perfumes. What for? She has to check that the products are really good quality. She's smelling a deodorant in the photo.

C Nancy's job is very important. She's a "page turner" at New York's Carnegie Hall. She has to turn the music pages for musicians. Why? The musicians are busy playing their instruments!

D This woman looks serious. Her name is Daniella and she's cleaning an animal bone. Can you guess her job? She's a "dinosaur duster". She has to dust dinosaur bones in a museum.

E Is this man holding a real snake? Yes. Larry is a "snake venom extractor". He takes poison out of snakes for laboratories.

Reading 🎧

Before you read

1 Look at the pictures. Do you know any of these jobs?

While you read

2 Read the article quickly. Match the photos with the texts.

1 _D_   2 ___   3 ___   4 ___   5 ___

After you read

3 Read the article again. Answer the questions.

1 What does Nam do? *He's a "golf ball diver".*
2 What's he doing in the photo?
3 What's Maria smelling in the photo?
4 What does Nancy do?
5 What's Daniella doing right now?
6 What does a "dinosaur duster" have to do?
7 What does Larry do?

Writing

1 Look at the Writing skills box.

Writing skills

Paragraphs

Develop one idea in each paragraph.

2 Now read the profile. Match the paragraph with the idea.

Usual activities _2_

Personal information ____

Interests ____

(1) Hi there! I'm 18 years old. My name is Marie, but my nickname is India. The reason? There are hundreds of "Maries" in the world. Do you have a nickname?

(2) I'm a student at Atlantic School in New Jersey in the United States. I usually get up very early, go to school and come home for lunch. In the afternoon I have to make my bed and put away my things. In the evening I usually meet my friends, or surf the Net.

(3) I love reading fashion magazines and listening to hip hop. Do you like rap or hip hop? Right now I'm listening to a new band called Klinical.

3 Fill in the chart with information about Marie.

Personal data	
Name	Country
Nickname	Town
Age	
Usual activities	
In the morning I _____	
In the afternoon I have to _____	
In the evening I _____	
Interests	**Activities right now**
I like _____	I'm _____ right now.

4 Now make notes about you.

5 Write your profile. Use the text and your notes to help you.

Speaking 🎧

1 Listen and read.

What kind of music do you like?

I like rock music.

What are you listening to right now?

I'm listening to Green Day. They're awesome.

What kind of books do you like?

What are you reading right now?

I like science fiction books.

I'm reading *Space Adventure*. It's exciting.

2 Look at the Pronunciation box. Listen to the examples.

Pronunciation

Stress

We usually stress verbs, nouns, and question words.

What kind of **music** do you **like**?

I like **rock music**.

Listen again and repeat.

3 Listen. Circle the stressed word(s) in each sentence.

1 (Where) do you (live)?
2 I'm a student.
3 I like swimming.
4 What kind of books do you like?

Now listen and repeat.

4 Practice the dialog with your partner.

5 Change the words in blue. Write a new dialog. Now practice the dialog in class.

Review 2

Vocabulary
Activities

1 Correct the verbs in the sentences.

1 I always ~~play~~ fast food.   _eat_
2 I usually watch to music.   _____
3 I never listen magazines.   _____
4 I l read climbing on the weekend. _____
5 I eat the drums in the evening.   _____
6 When do you paint to school?   _____

Household chores

2 Label the pictures with the chore.

1 _____put away_____   5 _____
2 _____   6 _____
3 _____   7 _____
4 _____   8 _____

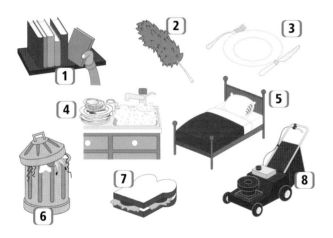

Grammar
Simple present and present progressive

1 Circle the correct form of the verbs.

Oscar is an opera singer. He (1) (works) / is working in Buenos Aires, Argentina. He usually (2) reads / is reading music and (3) practices / is practicing his part in the morning. Then, he (4) joins / is joining the other singers in the choir in the afternoon.
Right now all the singers (5) rehearse / are rehearsing *The Elixir of Love*, a comic opera. All the singers and dancers (6) wear / are wearing costumes and makeup. Oscar (7) stands / is standing on stage. He (8) plays / is playing the role of a man called Nemorino.

have to

2 Complete the sentences with *have to*, *has to*, *don't have to* or *doesn't have to*.

1 I'm a student. I _have to_ study, but I _don't have to_ teach.
2 They're actors. They _____ learn lines, but they _____ write movies.
3 She's a flight attendant. She _____ fly a plane. She _____ speak a foreign language.
4 He's a mechanic. He _____ work in an office. He _____ fix cars.
5 We're runners. We _____ train every day. We _____ use a computer.
6 You're a doctor. You _____ work with people, but you _____ work with animals.

Reading

The Elixir of Love

Nemorino is in love with Adina. He wants to marry her, but she is in love with another man, named Belcore. A man in town offers Nemorino a "love potion" with magical powers. Nemorino decides to buy the potion and give it to Adina. But the potion is really wine, and it doesn't work.
Nemorino is unhappy. He decides to join the army. He wants to earn some money and buy some MORE love potion.
While he is in the army Nemorino's uncle dies and leaves a fortune for him. Nemorino doesn't know he's rich now, but the town girls know.
When he comes back to the town, all the girls are interested in him because they know he has money. Nemorino is happy. He thinks the love potion is finally working!

1 Circle T (True) or F (False).

1 Nemorino loves Adina.   (T) / F
2 Adina doesn't love Belcore.   T / F
3 Nemorino buys wine from a man in town.   T / F
4 Nemorino joins the army to get more money.   T / F
5 He gets a lot of money when his uncle dies.   T / F
6 The girls like Nemorino because of the potion.   T / F

Different styles

Grammar: short comparative adjectives; long comparative adjectives
Vocabulary: physical appearance; personality

Introducing the topic

Vocabulary

1 Fill in the blanks in the descriptions with the words below.

> tight   loose   short   long   tall   straight
> curly   wavy   low   high

🎧 **Now listen and repeat.**

Recycling

2 What about you? Fill in your information below.

name: _____

height: _____

hair: _____

pants / jeans / skirt: _____

shirt / T-shirt / jacket: _____

shoes / boots: _____

① Cal

height: (1) *short*

hair: short and (2) _____

pants: long and (3) _____

shirt: loose

② Melina

height: short

hair: short and (4) _____

skirt: (5) _____

shirt: loose

boots: (6) _____

③ Denise

height: (7)_____

hair: long and (8) _____

jeans: long and (9) _____

jacket: short

shoes: (10) _____

Exploring the topic

Best friends, different styles

Kara and Tanya are best friends, but they have very different personalities and styles!

Kara likes going to the movies and reading. Her hair is shorter than Tanya's, and the color is lighter. Her hair is straighter, too. Her jeans are longer and tighter than Tanya's. Kara isn't taller than Tanya but her shoes are higher, and that makes a big difference.

Tanya is sporty and she likes skateboarding. Her hair is longer and darker than Kara's. Her jeans are shorter and looser than Kara's jeans and her T-shirt is tighter. Tanya wears lower shoes.

What do Kara and Tanya say about their different looks? Kara says: "Style is important for both of us. Your style says who you are. Styles aren't better or worse – they're just different." Tanya says: "Sure, we're best friends, but we're different people. You can see our personalities in our style."

Reading

1 Look at the photos and read the title. What is Kara and Tanya's relationship?

2 Read the text. Match the names with the photos.

Photo 1: _____   Photo 2: _____

3 🎧 Read and listen to the text again. Circle T (True) or F (False).

1   Kara's hair is lighter than Tanya. (T)/ F

2   Kara is taller than Tanya. T / F

3   Tanya is sporty. T / F

4   Tanya's jeans are tighter than Kara's. T / F

5   Kara and Tanya are both interested in style. T / F

6   Kara and Tanya have the same personality. T / F

Grammar

Short comparative adjectives

Talking about differences

1 Look at the chart.

adjective + -er + than

Mario is short**er than** Damon.

Mario's jeans are loos**er than** Damon's jeans.

Take note!

Spelling rules for short comparative adjectives

Regular

1 add -er or -r
   tall → taller
   long → longer
   loose → looser

2 ~~y~~ + -ier
   curly → curlier
   wavy → wavier

3 double consonant + -ier
   big → bigger

Irregular:
good → better
bad → worse

2 Fill in the blanks with the comparative form of the adjectives in parentheses.

1 Marla's hair is _shorter_ than my hair. (short)

2 Our house is _____ than your house. (big)

3 These jeans are _____ than my old jeans. (loose)

4 This book is _____ than that book. (funny)

5 The city is _____ than my village. (noisy)

6 My dog is _____ than your dog. (fat)

3 Look at the picture. Write complete sentences.

1 tree / tall / house

   _The tree is taller than the house_____.

2 truck / big / car

   _____.

3 cat / clean / dog

   _____.

4 motorcycle / fast / bus

   _____.

5 girl / tall / boy

   _____.

6 girl's hair / curly / boy's hair

   _____.

4 Find and correct the mistakes. (One mistake is a missing word).

1 David is tall than his mother. _taller_

2 My hair is darker your hair. _____

3 Your picture is gooder than my picture. _____

4 Jan's hair is curlyer than your hair. _____

5 My new jeans are biger than my old jeans.

   _____

6 The Canadian runner is fast than the Spanish runner. _____

Finished?
Page 105, Puzzle 3A

Over to you!

5 Say two things or people. Make a correct sentence to compare them. Use these ideas: movies, actors, singers, objects.

Student A: Tom Cruise and Brad Pitt.
Student B: Tom Cruise is shorter than Brad Pitt.

Building the topic

Vocabulary

1 Look at the pictures. Fill in the blanks with the words below.

> creative   competitive   sociable   helpful
> disorganized   talkative

🎧 **Now listen and repeat.**

2 🎧 Read and listen to the texts. Write the names of the people next to the statements.

1 His friend doesn't know where things are.
  Andrew

2 Her friend is interested in art and music.
  _____

3 His sister does things for other people. _____

4 Her brother always has something to say.
  _____

5 His friend likes being a winner. _____

6 His brother likes going to parties. _____

1 My brother Caleb is more _sociable_ than me. He has lots of friends, and he loves being with people.
Marcus, Sydney, Australia

2 My sister Katia is more _____ than most people. When you have a problem, she always helps you. She's great.
Dieter, Berlin, Germany

3 My friend Kayla is a great person. She's more _____ than me. She paints, writes poetry and plays the guitar.
Joni, Ontario, Canada

4 My friend Nick is more _____ than anyone I know. His room is a mess, and he can't find anything.
Andrew, Cape Town, South Africa

5 Luisa is my best friend. She's more _____ than my other friends. She plays tennis, runs and swims, and she always wants to win.
Adam, Curitiba, Brazil

6 My brother Carl is more _____ than anyone in our family. He never stops talking! Luckily, he's funny and interesting.
Melinda, Los Angeles, USA

Grammar

Long comparative adjectives

Talking about differences

1 Look at the chart.

more + adjective + than
Mario is **more** helpful **than** Damon.
Jan and Kim are **more** sociable **than** Karen.

2 Write sentences with the comparative form of the adjectives.

1 Kathy / helpful / Jim

   Kathy is more helpful than Jim .

2 This book / interesting / that book

   _____ .

3 Math / difficult / geography

   _____ .

4 Your jacket / colorful / my jacket

   _____ .

5 Your story / exciting / my story

   _____ .

6 My brother / talkative / my sister

   _____ .

3 Look at the information about Richmond Castle and the Alhambra. Fill in the blanks with the comparative form of the adjectives in parentheses.

RICHMOND CASTLE, YORKSHIRE, U.K.

The British started building the castle in 1071. The style is simple, and it is made of gray stone. It is not usually very crowded. It is located in the town of Richmond, Yorkshire. Tickets: $7.00.

THE ALHAMBRA, GRANADA, SPAIN

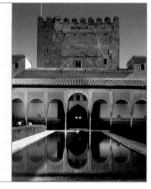

The Moors started building the palace in 1338. The buildings are colorful and very complicated. It is always very crowded. Tickets: $20.00.

1 The Alhambra is ___more crowded than___ Richmond Castle. (crowded)

2 Richmond Castle is _____ the Alhambra. (old)

3 The Alhambra is _____ Richmond Castle. (colorful)

4 The Alhambra is _____ Richmond Castle. (expensive)

5 The Alhambra's style is _____ Richmond Castle's style. (complicated)

6 Richmond Castle is _____ the Alhambra. (simple)

4 Look at the chart. Write sentences comparing the two activities.

	skiing	running
expensive		
exciting		
tiring		
dangerous		
difficult		
boring		

1 _Skiing is more expensive than running_ .

2 _____ .

3 _____ .

4 _____ .

5 _____ .

6 _____ .

Finished?
Page 105, Puzzle 3B

Over to you!

5 Say two activities. Make a correct sentence to compare them.

Student A: Swimming and scuba diving.

Student B: Scuba diving is more exciting than swimming.

Living English

Serious styling

Hip hop For boys and girls, pants are big and loose. Boys wear big, loose T-shirts. For girls, tops are smaller and tighter than boys' tops. This style is quite new, but it has a history. It began in the 1920s with zoot suits and jazz music.

Japanese Street This style is more interesting than other styles because everybody looks different – and everybody looks strange! The idea is to wear stranger clothes, have weirder makeup and more bizarre hairstyles than anyone else. You can look like an action hero, a fairy tale character or an alien. It's not easy to say exactly WHAT it is.

Grunge The grunge style is simpler and more practical than the other styles. The clothes are quite normal – just jeans and shirts, in plain colors. The grunge style is connected to grunge music, from the United States. It's easier than other styles. The clothes are cheaper and the look is more casual. Just don't wear anything very new – or very clean!

Punk Again, this style comes from a kind of music. The punk style is more difficult than other styles. It's really hard work! Punks have to color, cut and style their hair often. There are a lot of different clothes, but normally they are tighter and colors are darker than hip hop or grunge. Black is THE color. The makeup – for boys and girls – is really important.

Hippie This style is older than the others, and it comes back again and again. It comes from the late 1960s and it expresses the idea of freedom, peace and living with nature. The hippie style is more "artistic" than other styles. Clothes are very colorful, and there are usually lots of flowers and other patterns.

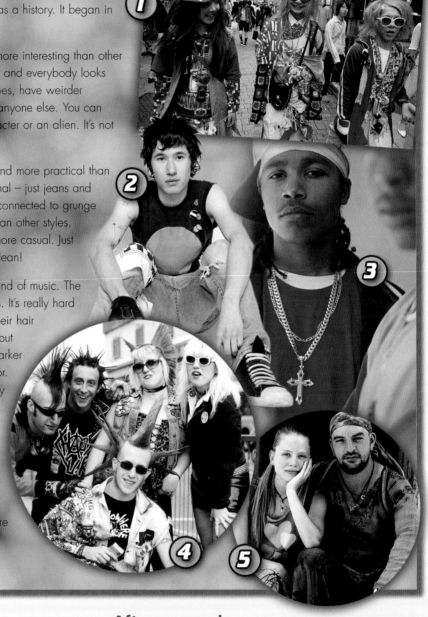

Reading 🎧

Before you read

1 Look at the pictures. What do you call these styles in your language?

While you read

2 Read the article. Match the pictures to the names of the styles.

Hip hop _3_   Japanese Street ___

Hippie ___   Grunge ___   Punk ___

After you read

3 Read the article again. Write the name of the style(s) next to the statements.

1 These styles are related to kinds of music.

   Hip hop _____ _____

2 This style is not easy to have. _____

3 This style started in the 1920s. _____

4 Bright colors are important in this style. _____

5 Makeup is important in these styles. _____

   _____

6 New clothes are not a part of this style. _____

Listening 🎧

1 Look at the Listening skills box.

Listening skills

Listening for key words

Key words are usually nouns, verbs or adjectives that help answer the questions.

Now look at the list of adjectives. Listen to the conversation. Check (✓) the adjectives you hear.

1 longer ✓   2 darker ___   3 taller ___

4 thinner ___   5 looser ___   6 tighter ___

7 colorful ___   8 bigger ___

2 Listen to the conversation again. Circle the correct word.

1 Amelia's hair is shorter / longer than Tina's.

2 Amelia is taller / shorter than Tina.

3 Amelia's jeans are looser / tighter than Tina's jeans.

4 Amelia's clothes are darker / more colorful than Tina's clothes.

5 Amelia's backpack is bigger / smaller than Tina's.

Writing

1 Read the text about Tomas's favorite person. Who is his favorite person? Name three good qualities his favorite person has.

My brother Carlos is my favorite person. He is older than I am – he's 18. He is taller than me and he is stronger. His hair is shorter than my hair, and his clothes are more fashionable. He always looks really good.

What I really like about Carlos is his personality. He is very sociable. He loves going to parties and going out with his friends. He is more honest than most people, too. He never tells lies. And he is more helpful than anyone else I know. He always does good things for people, and he always does them with a smile.

2 Fill in the chart with information about Carlos. Give examples of his qualities.

Name	Carlos
Age	18
Appearance	tall, strong
Personality	sociable – loves going to parties and going out with his friends

3 Now make notes about your favorite person.

4 Write about the person in exercise 3. Use the text and your notes to help you.

Review 3

Vocabulary
Physical appearance

1 Label the pictures with the correct adjectives.

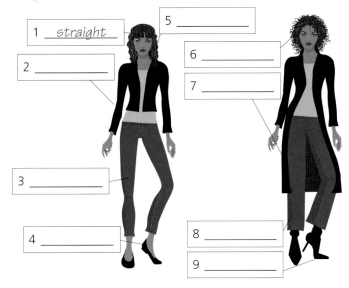

1 *straight*
2 _____
3 _____
4 _____
5 _____
6 _____
7 _____
8 _____
9 _____

Personality

2 Fill in the blanks with the correct adjectives.

1 Dana is very ___*creative*___. She paints, designs clothes and writes music.

2 I am so _____! I can't find anything in my room.

3 Julia loves going out with her friends. She's very _____.

4 José is more _____ than anyone I know. He is never quiet!

5 I'm not very _____. I do sports for fun, but I'm not interested in winning.

6 Tom is really _____. He always does nice things for his friends.

Grammar
Comparatives

1 Write comparative sentences using the adjectives in parentheses.

1 Tina is ___*taller than*___ Mario. (tall)

2 My hair is _____ Jo's. (long)

3 Greg's hair is _____ Rob's. (short)

4 Brad's jeans are _____ Jen's. (tight)

5 Mel's jeans are _____ than Lisa's. (loose)

6 Jim is _____ than Sharon. (happy)

2 Complete the e-mail with the correct comparative form of the adjectives in parentheses.

Hi Katie

Here I am at the National Track and Field Championship. It's (1) ___*more amazing than*___ (amazing) any other competition. All the athletes are (2) _____ (good) the runners in other races. They are (3) _____ (competitive) the runners at home, too. The weather is much (4) _____ (cold) the weather at home. That means warming up is (5) _____ (difficult) it normally is.

I'm (6) _____ (nervous) I usually am, but I'm running quite fast.

I'm (7) _____ (happy) I was yesterday because my speeds are really good today. Wish me luck!

Your friend,

Felicity

Study skills

Word families

When you learn a new word, you can find it in your dictionary and learn its "word family".

Look at the chart. *Create* is a verb, but you can also make *creative* (adjective) and *creation* (noun). This is its word family.

Now fill in the chart. Check your answers in the dictionary.

Verb	Adjective	Noun
create	creative	creation
organize	1 *organized*	2 _____
3 _____	4 _____	competition
5 _____	6 _____	help

4 On vacation

Grammar: *was / were*; simple past (affirmative)
Vocabulary: weather; vacation problems

Introducing the topic

Vocabulary

1 Label the weather symbols with the words below.

6 hot	☐ warm	☐ cold
☐ rainy	☐ windy	☐ sunny
☐ snowy	☐ icy	☐ cloudy

 Now listen and repeat.

Recycling

2 Describe the weather in your city.

Spring: _____

Summer: _____

Fall: _____

Winter: _____

Exploring the topic

Jody   Jeff

Jeff and Jody's travel diary

Nepal

We were in the Himalayas for a week.
It was snowy and the mountains were icy. We were 5000 meters up in the snow. It was very cold but the scenery was awesome. At night there was a snow storm. The next day we were back in our warm hotel rooms again.

Laos

The Buddha park in Vientiane was amazing. There was a statue of a big, reclining Buddha. It was very impressive. It was rainy, so we entered a temple. Inside there were little windows with lots of religious images. Soon it was sunny again and we were outside.

Indonesia

Indonesia was fun. Bali's beaches were beautiful and full of tourists. The weather was perfect. It was hot and sunny. That afternoon there was a Balinese dance group on the beach. It was really interesting. Later, we were in a famous temple called Tanah Lot. It's in the sea. It was windy and hot. Bali was interesting and fun.

Reading

1 Read Jeff and Jody's travel diary. Match the places with the attractions.

1 Nepal   a impressive building with religious images

2 Laos   b amazing beaches with interesting things to see and visit

3 Indonesia   c snowy mountains with beautiful scenery

2 Read and listen to the text. Write the name of the place(s).

1 The weather conditions were good in:
   _____

2 The weather conditions weren't good in:
   _____ and _____

3 Write the "weather journal".

1 The weather in Nepal was _snowy_ , _icy_ and _____.

2 The weather in Laos was _____ and _____.

3 The weather in Indonesia was _____, _____ and _____.

Grammar

was / were

Talking about the past

1 Look at the chart.

Affirmative	Negative
I / He / She / It **was** in Brazil last year.	I / He / She / It **wasn't** in Laos last year.
You / We / You / They **were** in Brazil last year.	You / We / You / They **weren't** in Laos last year.
There **was** a big temple.	There **wasn't** any snow.
There **were** mountains.	There **weren't** many tourists.

2 Circle the correct form of the verb in the sentences about Tibet.

1   Tibet (was) / were amazing.
2   Tibetan people was / were very friendly.
3   The weather was / were cold.
4   There was / were tall mountains and long rivers.
5   The Buddhist temple was / were impressive.
6   My friends and I was / were in Tibet for ten days.

New Zealand

Penguins and dolphins ✔
Beautiful lakes ✔
Pollution ✘
Temples ✘
A tower in Auckland ✔

3 Fill in the blanks with *There was*, *There were*, *There wasn't*, or *There weren't*.

1   *There were*   penguins and dolphins
2   _____ beautiful lakes.
3   _____ any pollution.
4   _____ any temples.
5   _____ a tower in Auckland.

4 Look at the chart.

Questions	Answers
Was I / he / she / it in Asia last year?	Yes, I / he / she / it **was**. / No, I / he / she / it **wasn't**.
Were you / we / you / they on vacation?	Yes, you / we / you / they **were**. / No, you / we / you / they **weren't**.
Was there a temple in Nepal?	Yes, there **was**. / No, there **wasn't**.
Were there many tourists?	Yes, there **were**. / No, there **weren't**.
Where were you last year?	I was in Nepal.
What was the weather **like**?	It was snowy and cold.

5 Kasia and Geri were on vacation together. Put the words in order to make questions for Geri.

1   you / in Africa / on your vacation / were?
    Were you in Africa on your vacation ?
2   like / the weather / what / was?
    _____ ?
3   were / you / when / there?
    _____ ?
4   Kasia / with you / was?
    _____ ?
5   any / special attractions / were there?
    _____ ?

6 Now match the questions from exercise 5 with the answers.

1   Last year. *3*
2   Yes, I was. ____
3   Yes, the Dragon Mountains were impressive. ____
4   It was hot and rainy. ____
5   Yes, she was. ____

Finished?
Page 107, Puzzle 4A

Over to you!

7 Imagine you were on vacation in an amazing place. Write a description of it.

Last year, I was in _____. The weather was (windy and cold). There were (wild animals / tall mountains/ buildings, …). There was a (big temple / a lion / …). We were there for ____ days. The vacation was (awesome, nice, fun, …).

Building the topic

Bad vacations

I was in Denmark with a group of friends. I ate some French fries in a fast food restaurant. Later, I felt sick. Ewwww!
Alex, 19

Last summer we went to Miami beach. But guess what happened? I fell out of the car and sprained my ankle.
Katherine, 16

Last winter my cousin and I went skiing in Portillo, a ski resort in Chile. The mountain was icy. Suddenly, I slipped and broke my leg. Too bad!
Javier, 18

Last winter my family and I went rafting in Montana. Our tour guide was really cute. He helped me onto the raft, but I fell over and hurt my knee. It was really embarrassing!
Kylie, 14

My cousin Sheila is a very active person. I'm not. On our last trip to Colorado we went trekking. I got eight blisters on each foot.
Olivia, 16

Last summer we went to Florida and there was a tornado. I was really scared and I fainted. The next day we went home. It was a very short vacation!
Antonio, 17

Vocabulary

1 Match the pictures to the verbs. Write the correct number next to the verbs.

☐ 1 sprain	☐ hurt	☐ slip
☐ get blisters	☐ feel sick	☐ faint

🎧 **Now listen and repeat.**

2 🎧 Read and listen to the text. Write the names next to the statements.

1 She hurt her knee. _Kylie_
2 He felt sick after eating French fries. _____
3 She went trekking and got blisters. _____
4 He fainted. _____
5 He slipped on a mountain. _____
6 She sprained her ankle in a beach resort. _____

Grammar
Simple past (affirmative)
Talking about the past

1 **Look at the chart.**

Regular		Irregular	
I / You / He / She / It	faint**ed**.	I / You / He / She / It	**felt** sick.
You / We / They	slipp**ed**.	You / We / They	**got** blisters.

Take note!

Regular verbs

Spelling rules

1 add -*ed*
   faint ➔ faint**ed**

2 add -*d*
   live ➔ lived

3 double consonant and add -*ed*
   slip ➔ slipped
   fall ➔ fell

4 change -*y* to -*i* and add -*ed*
   cr*y* ➔ cried

Irregular verbs don't follow a pattern.
break ➔ broke
get ➔ got

2 **Fill in the blanks with the simple past form of the verbs in parentheses. All the verbs are regular.**

1 Last year I _traveled_ to Florianopolis, in Brazil. (travel)

2 I _____ a backpack and surfing equipment. (carry)

3 I _____ at the airport for two hours. (wait)

4 I _____ in Brazil at eleven o'clock in the evening. (arrive)

5 In the morning I _____ Florianopolis, a beautiful town. (tour)

6 After midday, I _____ in the ocean. (surf)

7 At night I _____ in a dance club near the beach. (dance)

3 **Fill in the blanks with the past form of the verbs in parentheses.**

New Year trip to Norway

Monday
I spent New Year in Norway. I arrived on December 27th. I (1) _met_ (meet) my friend Gabriel at the airport. We went to a campsite and (2) _____ (stay) there for a week.
The first night I (3) _____ (have) dinner at the campsite under a sky full of stars.

Tuesday and Wednesday
I (4) _____ (go) to the Norwegian Fjords.

Thursday
I (5) _____ (climb) the mountains. My equipment was not very good. I (6) _____ (slip) and (7) _____ (fall) on the ice. But I was OK!

Friday
I (8) _____ (celebrate) New year with some friends in a restaurant on top of a mountain. Everything was fantastic.

Finished?
Page 107, Puzzle 4B

Over to you!

4 **Invent three problems that you had on vacation. Can the class guess how it happened?**

Student A: I broke my leg.
Student B: You went skiing and fell.
Student B: Yes. / No, I climbed a mountain.

Living English

The weather and you

1 Does your soccer injury hurt today? Is it stormy?

In 400 BC, Hippocrates wrote about the connection between the weather and the body.

In the 1870s, an American doctor, Sir Weir Mitchell, proved this connection was true. How? He observed many patients.

Lenny was one of Sir Mitchell's patients. He had a broken leg. Lenny felt strong pain with stormy weather. The pain stopped when the weather got better.

Fact: Stormy weather makes injuries hurt.

2 Do you feel happy or sad today? Is it sunny or cloudy?

We all know that bad weather makes you feel sad, and sunny days make you feel happy and energetic. But in the1950s Helmut Landsberg showed scientifically the connection between weather and feelings.

For example, many people in northern European countries feel sad in the winter. This is because there is little sun, and not many hours of daylight.

Fact: Bright sunshine makes you feel good.

3 Are you quick or slow today? Does cloudy weather make you slow? Some weather conditions slow down your reactions. For example, there are more car accidents on a wet day.

Fact: Wet or cloudy weather makes your reflexes slow.

4 Can you think fast today?

You can think fast during hurricanes and thunderstorms. Why? Because your adrenaline goes up. But very cold or very hot temperatures make you think slowly.

For example, students do worse on tests when it's very hot or very cold.

Fact: Your mind works fast in high pressure, and comfortable temperatures.

Reading 🎧

Before you read

1 What kind of weather makes you feel happy? What kind of weather makes you feel sad?

While you read

2 Look at the Reading skills box.

Reading skills

Getting the general idea

To get the general idea of a text, first read quickly and don't stop for difficult words.

Now read the text quickly. Match the topics to the paragraphs.

1 The weather and your reflexes.   Paragraph _3_

2 The weather and your mind.   Paragraph ____

3 The weather and your pain.   Paragraph ____

4 The weather and your feelings.   Paragraph ____

After you read

3 Circle T (True) or F (False).

1 Hippocrates was the first person to write about the connection between the weather and the body.   (T)/ F

2 Dr Mitchell proved the connection between weather and pain.   T / F

3 Dr Helmut Landsberg didn't find any connection between weather and feelings.   T / F

4 People in northern European countries feel sad in the summer.   T / F

5 There are more accidents on a wet day.   T / F

6 Very cold temperatures help your mind work faster.   T / F

Listening 🎧

1 **Look at the photos. Label the photos with the words below.**

> dogsled   Eskimo   snowmobile

1

snowmobile

2

_____

3

_____

2 **Listen. Check (✓) the topics they talk about.**

weather ✓   houses   food
clothes   jobs   transportation

3 **Listen again. Circle a or b.**

1   Eskimos live in the Arctic Circle in
   a   Alaska, Canada and Greenland
   ⓑ   Alaska, Canada and Iceland

2   In the Arctic Circle, the temperature is
   a   from zero to −60°C   b   from zero to −70°C

3   An igloo is a house made of
   a   wood   b   snow

4   In the past Eskimos ate a lot of
   a   fish and meat   b   vegetables

5   Nowadays, Eskimos travel by
   a   snowmobile   b   dogsled

Speaking 🎧

1 **Listen and read.**

> How was your vacation?
> Great. I went to New Zealand for ten days.
> Cool. What was the weather like?
> It was cloudy and windy.
> How was your vacation?
> Great. I went trekking in South America.
> What was it like?
> It was very exciting. But I got blisters on my feet.

2 **Look at the Pronunciation box. Listen to the examples.**

Pronunciation

'd' and 'th' sounds

'd' and *'th'* are different sounds.

/d/	/ð/
day	they
clouds	clothes

Now listen and repeat.

3 **Listen. Put the words in the correct column.**

> than   Dan   dose   those   there   dare

/d/	/ð/
	than

4 **Practice the dialog with your partner.**

5 **Change the words in blue. Write a new dialog. Now practice the dialog in class.**

Review 4

Vocabulary

Weather

1 Find eight weather words.

cloudy hotrainy warmicy coldsunnysnowy

Holiday problems

2 Fill in the blanks with the words below.

> sprained   fainted   slipped   got blisters
> hurt   felt sick

1 On Tuesday I _sprained_ my ankle.

2 On Wednesday I had a heavy lunch and I _____ .

3 On Thursday I bought new shoes. I _____ on both feet.

4 On Friday I played hockey and I _____ my knee.

5 On Saturday night I went to a pop concert but it was so hot that I _____ .

6 On Sunday I _____ on the ice and fell.

Grammar

was / were

1 Fill in the blanks with *was* or *were*.

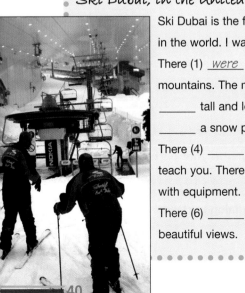

Ski Dubai, in the United Arab Emirates

Ski Dubai is the first indoor ski resort in the world. I was there last month. There (1) _were_ ski slopes with mountains. The mountains (2) _____ tall and looked real. There (3) _____ a snow park with games. There (4) _____ ski instructors to teach you. There (5) _____ a shop with equipment. There (6) _____ also two cafes with beautiful views.

Simple past (affirmative)

2 Fill in the blanks with the simple past form of the verbs in parentheses.

In the morning my friends and I went to the Snow School. We (1) _started_ (start) our day with our first ski lesson. Skiing is not easy, so we (2) _____ (fall) over hundreds of times. We all laughed and had fun. After the ski lesson we (3) _____ (go) shopping. We (4) _____ (buy) skis and snow boots. At about midday we were tired and hungry so we (5) _____ (have) lunch at St Moritz. After lunch we (6) _____ (visit) the snow park. We (7) _____ (play) games and (8) _____ (throw) snowballs at each other. Dubai was the coolest experience of my life.

Reading

1 Read the text. Circle T (True) or F (False).

⮊ Monterey Bay Aquarium

Monterey Bay Aquarium was educational and fun. There was marine life from all over the world. There were good exhibits, interactive games and information about the environment.

⮊ We saw whales and seals through the window of the Portola Café.

⮊ Don't miss the octopus and shark exhibits. They are a 'must-see'. We saw a white shark at feeding time. It was fascinating and entertaining.

⮊ It's good to visit Monterey Bay Aquarium in the summer with warm, sunny weather to really enjoy the aquarium experience.

1 At the aquarium there is information about the environment. ⓣ/ F

2 She thinks the octopus and shark exhibits were great. T / F

3 He saw seals, whales, penguins, sharks, and octopuses. T / F

4 He saw a white shark eating. T / F

5 It's good to visit the aquarium in the winter. T / F

5 Music world

Grammar: simple past (*yes* / *no* questions and negatives); simple past (*wh-* questions)
Vocabulary: musical instruments; biography verbs

Introducing the topic

1 Stacey Ferguson
2 Guy Berryman Coldplay
3 Alicia Keys
4 Tré Cool Green Day
5 The Edge U2
6 Jonny Greenwood Radiohead

Vocabulary

1 Match the photos with the words below.
Write the correct number next to the words.

- 5 guitar
- ☐ bass
- ☐ drums
- ☐ keyboard
- ☐ piano
- ☐ microphone

🎧 **Now listen and repeat.**

Recycling

2 Fill in the blanks with the correct names.

1 _Stacey Ferguson_ is a singer.
2 _____ is a guitarist.
3 _____ is a drummer.
4 _____ is a keyboard player.
5 _____ is a bass guitarist.
6 _____ is a pianist.

Exploring the topic

Legends and contemporary bands

The Rolling Stones

Today, pop music is an important part of our culture. But before the 1950s, people didn't listen to rock or pop. Modern music started with rock 'n' roll, and now we have many different styles of pop music.

Led Zeppelin

Rock

Red Hot Chili Peppers, The Killers and U2 are some of today's rock bands. The Rolling Stones formed the first famous rock band in 1963. They didn't like the pop music of the 1960s. They wanted to play "noisier", harder rock. They were the "bad guys" of rock.

The Clash

Aretha Franklin

Heavy metal

Ozzy Osborne is a famous heavy metal singer and TV star. He made his first record in 1970 with his band Black Sabbath.

Did heavy metal start with Ozzy?
No, it didn't. Led Zeppelin made the first heavy metal record in 1968.

Punk

Green Day plays punk music. Punk is fast, simple rock music.

Did other groups play punk music before Green Day?
Yes, they did. Punk started in England in 1976. Some punk music was violent, but one group, The Clash, didn't sing violent songs. They sang about social problems.

Soul

Joss Stone is a soul singer. Some singers, for example Alicia Keys and Beyoncé, mix soul with hip hop.
These singers didn't make the first soul records. The "Queen of Soul" was Aretha Franklin. She was famous in the 1960s.

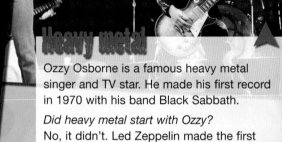
The Fatback Band

Rap

Snoop Dogg and Eminem are rappers. Rap became very popular in the 1990s, but it didn't start then. The Fatback Band made the first rap record in 1979.

Reading

1 Read the text. Circle T (True) or F (False).

1 Rock music started with bands like Radiohead and Coldplay.   T /(F)

2 Led Zeppelin started heavy metal in 1968.   T / F

3 Green Day was the first punk band.   T / F

4 Alicia Keys and Beyoncé mix soul with hip hop.   T / F

5 Rap started in the 1990s.   T / F

2 🎧 Read and listen to the text again. Complete the chart.

Music style	Contemporary band / singer	Legendary band / singer
Rock	Red Hot Chili Peppers, The Killers, U2	The Rolling Stones
(1) *Heavy metal*	Ozzy Osborne	(2) _____
Punk	(3) _____	(4) _____
(5) _____	Beyoncé	(6) _____
(7) _____	(8) _____	The Fatback Band

Grammar

Simple past (*yes* / *no* questions)

Asking about the past

1 Look at the chart.

Questions	Short answers
Did I / you / he / she / it **buy** a record yesterday?	Yes, I / you / he / she / it **did**. / No, I / you / he / she / it **didn't**.
Did we / you / they **play** soul music?	Yes, we / you / they **did**. / No, we / you / they **didn't**.

2 Look at Green Day's fact file. Put the words in order to make questions. Then write the answers.

Green Day **fact file**

Formed: 1988   In: Berkeley, California

Music style: **punk rock**

Awards: Grammy for Best Alternative Music Performance 1994

First hit: The album *Dookie* sold 10 million copies

Popular events: Played at Woodstock in 1994

Records: *Holiday* 2005, *Boulevard of Broken Dreams* 2005

1   Green Day / start playing / in 1988 / Did?

   Did Green Day start playing in 1988 ?

   Yes, they did .

2   the band / form / Did / in New York?

   _____?

   _____.

3   the band / Did / in 2004 / record *Holiday*?

   _____?

   _____.

4   the album *Dookie* / sell a lot of copies / Did?

   _____?

   _____.

5   the band / in 1996 / win an award / Did?

   _____?

   _____.

6   the band / Did / in 1994 / play at Woodstock?

   _____?

   _____.

3 Look at the chart.

Negative
I / You / He / She / It **didn't win** an award in 1994.
We / You / They **didn't play** hip hop.

4 Correct the information in red. Then write the true sentences with the words in parentheses.

1   Jimi Hendrix played the drums. (guitar)

   He didn't play the drums. He played the

   guitar .

2   The Beatles played punk rock. (pop rock)

   _____

   _____.

3   Eminem recorded Slim Shady in 2005. (Curtain Call)

   _____

   _____.

4   Maroon 5 started playing in 1985. (1999)

   _____

   _____.

5   Alicia Keys grew up in London. (New York)

   _____

   _____.

6   Coldplay formed in 2002. (1998)

   _____

   _____.

Finished?
Page 107, Puzzle 5A

Over to you!

5 Ask your partner four questions about the past with *Did you ...* ? Use the verbs below.

e-mail a friend   watch a good movie   go out
wear a new T-shirt   buy a new CD

Student A: Did you e-mail a friend last weekend?
Student B: Yes, I did. / No, I didn't.

Building the topic

Vocabulary

1 Read about pop singer Joss Stone. Fill in the blanks in the questions with the words below.

> grow up   win an award   record an album
> start her career   sign a contract   was born
> have a hit record   become famous

🎧 Now listen and repeat.

2 🎧 Read and listen to the text. Then listen again and repeat the questions.

A When _was_ she _born_?
She was born on April 11th, 1987.

B Where did she _____ _____?
She grew up in Devon, U.K.

C How did she _____ _____ _____?
She appeared on a TV talent contest *Star for a Night* at the age of fourteen.

D When did she _____ __ _____?
She signed a contract in 2002.

E When did she _____ _____ _____?
She recorded her first album *The Soul Sessions* in 2004. It sold two million copies.

F How did she _____ _____?
She became famous with her first album in 2004.

G When did she _____ __ _____ _____?
She had her first hit record with *Fell in love with a boy* in 2004.

H When did she _____ _____ _____?
She won Best British Female in the 2004 Brit awards.

3 Match the answers for Shakira with the questions A–H from the text about Joss Stone.

1 She won a lot of talent contests in Colombia when she was ten. _C_

2 She recorded her first album *Magia* when she was only fourteen. ___

3 In Barranquilla, Colombia. ___

4 She won a Grammy for Best Female Pop Vocal in 2000. ___

5 She had her first hit record with *Estoy aquí*. ___

6 February 2nd, 1977. ___

7 She became internationally famous with her record *Whenever, Wherever* in 2001. ___

8 She signed a contract in 1990. ___

Grammar

Simple past (*wh-* questions)

Asking about the past

1 Look at the chart.

wh- questions
What did you do last night?
Where did he go on vacation?
When did she record an album?
Why did they win an award?
How did you start your career?
How many records did they sell?

2 Circle the correct question word.

1 (Who)/ Where is Natasha Bedingfield? She is a pop singer.

2 Where / When was she born? In 1981.

3 Where / How was she born? In London.

4 How / Why did she start her career? She started singing with her brother Daniel.

5 Who / What was her first hit? The album *Unwritten*.

6 What / Why does she do in her free time? She meets her family and friends.

3 Read Beyoncé's profile. Put the words in order to make questions.

1 Was /she / born / When
   When was she born ?

2 did / Where / start singing / she
   _____ ?

3 Destiny's Child / its first album / When / did / record
   _____ ?

4 did / sell / How many albums / Destiny's Child
   _____ ?

5 When / a MTV Award / Destiny's Child / did / win
   _____ ?

4 Read Beyoncé's profile. Match the questions with the answers from exercise 3.

Beyoncé profile

Name: Beyoncé Giselle Knowles

She was born on September 4th, 1981 in Houston, Texas.

She started singing at the age of 7 in a church choir.

In 1998 Destiny's Child recorded its first album.

In ten years the group sold 33 million albums.

In 2005 the group won a MTV award.

A   33 million. _4_

B   In 2005. ____

C   In 1981. ____

D   In 1998. ____

E   In a church choir. ____

5 Make the questions about Beyoncé. Use *When did she first / last ... ?*

1 _When did she first act_ in a movie?
   She first acted in a movie in 2002.

2 _____ in public?
   She first sang in public at the age of seven

3 _____ ?
   She last recorded with Destiny's Child in 2002.

4 _____ as a solo artist?
   She first recorded as a solo artist in 2003 with *Dangerously in Love*.

Finished?
Page 107, Puzzle 5B

Over to you!

6 Ask your partner questions with *When did you first / last ... ?* Use the verbs below.

ride a bike	stay at a friend's house
go to a costume party	go on vacation
play a game	go to a party

Student A: When did you first ride a bike?
Student B: When I was five years old.

Living English

Virtual bands

Gorillaz is an example of a virtual band. The members are animated characters, not real people. The real musicians record the songs in a studio.

Noodle Russel 2D Murdoc

Gorillaz

Gorillaz is a British virtual band. They play a mixture of rap, rock and hip hop.

The band has four animated characters.
– 2D is the singer and keyboard player.
– Murdoc is the bass guitarist.
– Noodle is the guitarist and singer.
– Russel is the drummer.

But, the REAL singer-songwriter Damon Albarn created the group.

History of Gorillaz
This band has a virtual history. Why is it virtual? Because Damon Albarn invented it.

2D was a keyboard player. He worked in a music store. One day, a man called Murdoc went into the music store. He stole a keyboard and accidentally hurt 2D's eye.
After the accident, Murdoc took care of 2D and they became friends.

Murdoc had a dream. He wanted to form a successful band. Murdoc and 2D started the band. 2D was the singer and the keyboard player for the band.

Murdoc found the drummer, Russel, in a rap music store in London. Russel was from the U.S. and he had a lot of friends who were rappers.

The group needed a guitarist. They put an ad in a music magazine. That day they received a big package from Japan. They opened the package and a girl with a guitar appeared. Her name was Noodle.

Finally, in 1998 Gorillaz gave a concert. A man from a record company walked onto the stage and asked Gorillaz to sign a contract.

They recorded their first album, *Gorillaz*, in 2001. It sold more than a million and a half copies.

Reading 🎧

Before you read

1 Look at the picture. Do you know this band?

While you read

2 Read the text. Match 1–4 with A–D.

1 A virtual band is
2 Gorillaz is
3 The band's history is
4 Damon Albarn

A is a real person. He created Gorillaz.

B not real. Damon Albarn invented it.

C a music band with animated characters.

D a British virtual band.

After you read

3 Read the text again and put the events in order.

Murdoc found the drummer, Russel, in a rap music store. ____

Gorillaz recorded their first album. ____

Noodle, the guitarist, came in a package from Japan. ____

The band signed a contract. ____

The band gave a concert. ____

Murdoc hurt 2D's eye in a music store. _1_

Murdoc took care of 2D. ____

Writing

1 Look at the Writing skills box.

Dates and time expressions

Use dates and time expressions to make the order of events clear.

Dates: On July 2nd, 1977

In 1990

Time expressions: When she was six, two years later, after

2 Now read the biography. Circle the dates and time expressions.

A biography: Damon Albarn

Damon is the singer-songwriter in Gorillaz. He was born on (March 23rd, 1968) in East London, England, but he grew up in Colchester. He started playing the violin and the piano when he was twelve. After high school, he studied drama. He didn't like acting, and he started writing music.

He went to London in 1987 and he worked as a tea boy in a studio. He worked on his music at night.

A year later, he formed a band, Circus, with his old school friend, Graham Coxon. They signed a contract and became Blur. Damon formed Gorillaz in 1999.

3 Fill in the chart with information about Damon Albarn.

Singer	Date and time expressions	Event
Damon Albarn	On March 23rd, 1968 When he was 12 After high school In 1987 A year later In 1999	was born

4 Now make notes about a singer that you like.

5 Write the biography of the person in exercise 4. Use the text and your notes to help you.

Speaking 🎧

1 Listen and read.

2 Look at the Pronunciation box. Listen to the examples.

Questions

Intonation goes up (↗) at the end of *yes / no* questions and down (↘) at the end of *wh-* questions.

What did you do yesterday? ↘ Did you have a good time? ↗

Listen again and repeat.

3 Put ↗ or ↘ .

1 Where did you go on vacation?

2 Did you go out last night?

3 Did she win an award?

4 Where did she grow up?

Listen and check.

4 Practice the dialog with your partner.

5 Change the words in blue. Write a new dialog. Now practice the dialog in class.

Review 5

Vocabulary
Musical instruments

1 Write the correct instrument.

1 _microphone_
2 _____
3 _____
4 _____
5 _____
6 _____

Biography verbs

2 Fill in the blanks with the phrases below.

> signed a contract   started her career   grew up
> was born   won   became famous

Keira Knightley is a British actress. She (1) _was born_
on March 26th, 1985 in England. She (2) _____
in London. She (3) _____ at the age of nine in a
film called *A Village Affair* (1994). She (4) _____
with Walt Disney for a movie called *Princess of
Thieves*. She (5) _____ with *Pirates of the
Caribbean* in 2003. She (6) _____ a Best Actress
Golden Globe award, for *Pride and Prejudice* in 2006.

Grammar
Simple past (*yes / no* questions)

1 Read the Keira Knightley text again. Write the
questions and answers.

1 _Did she grow up_ (grow up) in London?
   Yes, she did.

2 _____ (start her career) at the age
   of ten? _____.

3 _____ (sign a contract) with Walt
   Disney? _____.

4 _____ (become famous) with
   Pirates of the Caribbean? _____.

5 _____ (win an award) for *Princess
   of Thieves*? _____.

Simple past (*wh-* questions)

2 Write questions about
Joaquin Phoenix. Use the
underlined part of the
answers to help you.

1 Where _was he born_ ?
   He was born in San Juan,
   Puerto Rico.

2 When _____
   _____?
   He was born on October
   28th, 1974.

3 How _____?
   He started his career in TV commercials.

4 Where _____?
   He grew up in South America and the U.S.

5 How _____?
   He became famous in *Gladiator*.

6 When _____?
   He won an award in 2005 for *Walk the Line*.

Study skills

English outside the classroom

English is everywhere!

1 Match the pictures with the places you can
see or hear English.

> stores [2]   song lyrics [ ]   signs [ ]
> movies [ ]   advertisements [ ]

2 Try to find ten English words outside the
classroom and write them in your notebook.

6 The coolest places

Grammar: superlative adjectives; *have to / can't*; *don't have to / can*
Vocabulary: describing a place; travel activities

Introducing the topic

Vocabulary

1 Match the pictures with the words below. Write the correct number next to the words.

7 crowded	☐ deep	☐ large
☐ long	☐ narrow	☐ small
☐ tall	☐ wide	

🎧 Now listen and repeat.

Recycling

2 Think of an example of each of the following things in your country.

1 a tall building (for example, the Empire State Building)

2 a long river (for example, the Nile)

3 an interesting museum (for example, the Louvre)

4 a famous lake (for example, Lake Michigan)

Exploring the topic

Reading

1 **Look at the pictures. Do you know any of the places? What do you know about them?**

2 **Read and listen to the text. Write the correct letter next to the statements.**

1 It is between Argentina and Uruguay. ___F___
2 It has 101 floors. _____
3 It goes to the top of Mount Niesen. _____
4 It is almost 2 kilometers deep. _____
5 It is a country in a city. _____
6 It is now much bigger than it was. _____
7 It has many people in a small area. _____

A
Manila, in the Philippines, is the most crowded city in the world. It has 41,282 people per square kilometer.

B
The tallest building in the world is in Taipei, in Taiwan. It is called Taipei 101. It has 101 floors and is 509 meters tall.

C
Vatican City in Rome is the smallest independent state in the world. It has a population of 920, and it is only 0.44 square kilometers.

Amazing facts
– read and be amazed!

D
The longest staircase in the world is the staircase on Mount Niesen in Switzerland. It has 11,674 steps to the top of the mountain, which is 2,336 meters high.

E
The deepest lake in the world is Lake Baikal in Siberia, Russia. It is 1,637 meters deep. That's almost 2 kilometers!

F
The Rio de la Plata is the widest river in the world. It is on the border between Argentina and Uruguay, and at its widest point, it is 220 kilometers wide.

G
The City Montessori School is the largest school in the world. It is in Lucknow, India, and it opened in 1959 with five students. Today it has over 25,000 students!

Grammar

Superlative adjectives

Talking about unique things

1 Look at the chart.

the + superlative + noun
Taipei 101 is **the** tall**est** building in the world.
Manila is **the most crowded** city in the world.

Take note!

Spelling rules for superlative adjectives

Short adjectives

1 add *-est* or *-st*

   tall → the tallest

   large → largest

2 ~~y~~ + *-iest*

   crazy → the craziest

3 double consonant + *-iest*

   big → the biggest

Long adjectives

interesting → the most interesting

Irregular

good → the best

bad → the worst

2 Circle the correct form.

1 Anthony is the (shortest) / most short boy in the class.

2 I think London is the interesting / most interesting city in the world.

3 The Great Wall is the most biggest / biggest man-made object in the world.

4 This restaurant has the worst / baddest food in town.

5 Kendra is fastest / the fastest runner on the team.

3 Look at the pictures. Fill in the blanks with the superlative form of the adjectives below.

young	crowded	difficult
good	scary	tall

1 Andy is _the tallest_ person in the class.

2 This is _____ _____ exercise in the test.

3 This is _____ _____ classroom in the school.

4 *The Dead Alive* is _____ movie in the world!

6 Dana is _____ _____ person in our family. She's ten months old.

6 The day he won the prize was _____ _____ day of Pedro's life.

4 Write sentences with the comparative or superlative. Use the words in parentheses.

1 _Jammy's is the best restaurant in our city_ . (Jammy's / good restaurant / in our city)

2 _____. (Kelly / tall / Dawn)

3 _____. (my village / beautiful place / in the country)

4 _____. (Jan's school / big / her brother's school)

5 _____. (Everest / high mountain / in the world)

6 _____. (my MP3 player / expensive / your DVD player)

Finished?
Page 107, Puzzle 6A

Over to you!

5 Say the name of a person or place. Another student makes a correct superlative sentence.

Student A: Shakira

Student B: Shakira is the more famous singer in the United States.

Student A: Sorry – it isn't a correct sentence.

Student C: Shakira is the best singer in the world.

Student A: Yes! Your turn.

Building the topic

The Great Wall of China

You have to follow the rules at the Great Wall.
* You have to carry your passport all the time.
* You can sleep in the guard towers, but you can't camp outdoors.
* You can't drop litter. You have to take it away.
* You don't have to take a tour. You can go on your own, but read about it before you go.
* You have to buy a ticket to visit the Great Wall.
* You can bargain for souvenirs, but you can't use a credit card. You have to pay in cash!

$20!
$10?

RULES

Vocabulary

1 Match the pictures with the words below. Write the correct number next to the words.

6 take a tour		follow the rules
buy a ticket		carry your passport
camp		use a credit card
drop litter		bargain

🎧 Now listen and repeat.

2 🎧 Read and listen to the text. Circle T (True) or F (False).

1 You don't have to carry your passport.   T / **F**

2 You can't camp outdoors.   T / F

3 You can use a credit card to pay for souvenirs.   T / F

4 You have to take a tour.   T / F

5 You have to buy a ticket.   T / F

Grammar

have to / can't

Talking about rules

1 **Look at the chart.**

Necessary	Forbidden
You **have to** carry your passport.	You **can't** camp outdoors.
You **have to** buy a ticket.	You **can't** drop litter.

2 **Circle the correct form.**

1 You can't / have to smoke here! It's forbidden.

2 We have to / can't wear uniforms to school. Normal clothes are not okay.

3 "Do you have to / Can't you go now?" "Yes, I do. I'm late for school!"

4 You can't / have to use a credit card in this store. They don't accept them.

5 We have to / can't go to the airport now! The plane leaves in an hour.

don't have to / can

Talking about choices

3 **Look at the chart.**

Not necessary	Possible
You **don't have to** go on an organized tour.	You **can** sleep in the guard towers.
We **don't have to** wear a school uniform.	We **can** wear what we want to school.

4 **Look at the pictures of Crazy School. Fill in the blanks with *can*  or *don't have to* and the correct verb below.**

have   skate   take   choose   give   wear

1 You *don't have to* wear a uniform.

2 You _____ your classes outside.

3 You _____ inside the school.

4 You _____ tests.

5 You _____ which classes you want to go to.

6 You _____ a report card to your parents – there aren't any!

Finished?
Page 107, Puzzle 6B

Over to you!

5 **Make a sign showing a rule for your school. Show it to the class. Can the class guess the rule? Use *have to* or *can't*.**

Student A: Here's my sign. What does it mean?
Student B: You have to ride a bike in the school.
Student A: No, that isn't correct.
Student C: You can't ride a bike in the school.
Student A: That's right. Your turn.

Living English

YOUTH TRAVEL

Reading 🎧

Before you read

1 Look at the photos and the title of the article. What is the article about?

1 My dad is in the army, so we visit lots of different countries. For me, the coolest city for young people is definitely Glasgow, in Scotland. Glasgow has the best music scene in the world, and it has the greatest museums, parks and galleries too. It's the best city for sports – especially soccer and rugby. What's the worst thing about Glasgow? It's quite expensive, so you have to spend a lot of money.
Bryan, Virginia, USA

2 Gothenburg, in Sweden, is definitely the coolest city in Europe. (It's one of the coldest, too!) It is the most beautiful and most varied city in Sweden, and it's Scandinavia's largest port. You don't have to have a lot of money to stay in Gothenburg, and you can find lots of free or cheap things to do. There are a lot of students in the city, so the music and arts scene is really exciting. You don't have to travel far to enjoy nature, and winter sports are very popular. Just remember to wear lots of warm clothes in the winter!
Annika, Gothenburg, Sweden

3 My favorite place is Cancun, in Mexico. It's the best place in the world for young people. You can do everything there: go to great beaches, meet cool people and eat the best food in Mexico. The worst thing about Cancun is the number of people who visit, especially in the spring. It's crowded at that time of the year, so you have to stay away from the most popular places.
Rosa, Mexico City, Mexico

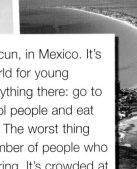

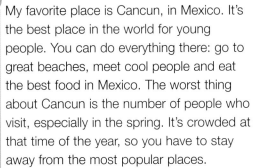

While you read

2 Look at the Reading skills box.

Reading skills

Finding specific information

To find specific information, learn to find the nouns in a text quickly.

You have two minutes. Look quickly at the whole text and write the number of the paragraph(s) where you find the nouns.

1 students _2_
2 sports ____ and ____
3 beaches ____
4 music ____ and ____
5 museums ____

After you read

3 Read the article again. Write the names of the places next to the statements.

1 It is a good place for sports. _Glasgow_
2 You don't have to have a lot of money to enjoy the place. _____
3 It is very crowded at certain times of the year. _____
4 It has nice beaches. _____
5 Activities there cost a lot of money. _____
6 It has very cold weather during part of the year. _____

Listening 🎧

1 Listen to the conversation. Who has a new school: Tim or Katy?

2 Listen again. Circle T (True) or F (False).

1 Katy is happy at her new school.   **T**/ F

2 Katy can wear whatever she wants to school. T / F

3 Katy thinks the teachers are very good.   T / F

4 Tim thinks Katy doesn't have much
homework.   T / F

5 Katy has to take a lot of tests.   T / F

6 Katy enjoys doing projects.   T / F

Writing

1 Read the brochure. Where is the place? Name three reasons why it's a good place to visit.

Are you planning your next vacation? Come to Oaxaca, the most beautiful place on earth!

Oaxaca is one of the most amazing places in Mexico. It has some of the highest mountains, the most beautiful beaches and the friendliest people. The climate is wonderful, the food is delicious and the shopping is incredible.

A few tips for travelers:

Money
You can spend American dollars or Mexican pesos. You can bargain for cheaper prices in the street market.

Drink
You can't drink the tap water. You have to drink bottled water.

Weather
You don't have to bring warm clothes. Temperatures are always 20ºC or higher. You have to wear sunscreen because it's very easy to get a sunburn.

Plan your trip to Oaxaca now!
It's the best vacation spot in the world!

2 Fill in the chart with information about Oaxaca.

General	Tips
highest mountains, most beautiful beaches, friendliest people, wonderful climate, _____, _____	Money: American dollars / Mexican pesos, _____ Drink: _____, _____ Weather: _____, _____

3 Now make notes about a place that you know.

4 Write a brochure about the place in exercise 3. Use the text and your notes to help you.

Review 6

Vocabulary

Describing a place

1 Fill in the missing letters in the adjectives.

1 s m a l l
2 _ i _ e
3 _ a _ _ e
4 _ a _ _ o _
5 _ a _ _
6 _ _ o _ _ e _
7 _ e e _
8 _ o _ _

Travel activities

2 Label the pictures with the travel activities.

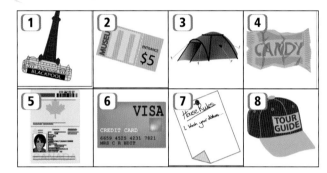

1 bargain
2 _____
3 _____
4 _____
5 _____
6 _____
7 _____
8 _____

Grammar

Superlatives

1 Fill in the blanks with the correct superlative form of the adjectives in parentheses.

1 The longest (long) street in the world (1,900 kilometers) starts in Toronto, Canada.

2 _____ (wide) street in the world is in Buenos Aires. It is 140 meters wide.

3 _____ (small) park in the world is in Portland, Oregon. It is only 0.29 square meters!

4 _____ (expensive) movie is *King Kong* (2005). It cost $207 million to make.

5 Monaco is _____ (crowded) country in the world, with 42,649 people per square mile.

6 _____ (fast) speed on a skateboard is 100.66 kilometers per hour!

have to / can't

2 Write sentences with *have to* or *can't* about the Tate Modern Gallery.

1 You can't take photographs .
(take photographs ✗)

2 _____.
(check large bags ✓)

3 _____.
(leave young children alone ✗)

4 _____.
(touch the works of art ✗)

5 _____.
(arrive at least 30 minutes before closing ✓)

6 _____.
(buy tickets for special exhibits ✓)

don't have to / can

3 Fill in the blanks with *don't have to* or *can*.

1 I can come home at 11:00 p.m., but if I'm late my mom gets mad!

2 We _____ wear a uniform. We can wear our own clothes.

3 You _____ take tests at my school. You can do projects.

4 I _____ go to bed later on the weekend.

Reading

ANTARCTIC CRUISE

For the most unusual experience of your life, try an Antarctic cruise. You can see the most amazing scenery on earth, including mountains, icebergs and snowy "deserts".
You have to go in the Antarctic summer – November through March – because the weather is too cold at other times. You can see the most interesting animals on earth, including great whales and hundreds of seals and penguins!
Tours start in the far south of Argentina, so combine your Antarctic trip with a visit to this beautiful country and you can experience the most unforgettable vacation of your life.

1 Answer the questions.

1 What place is the article about? *The Antarctic*

2 How can you visit the place?

3 When do you have to go there?

4 What animals can you see?

5 What country can you also visit as part of your trip?

7 Crime scene

Grammar: past progressive (affirmative / negative); past progressive (questions)
Vocabulary: conflict verbs; places

Introducing the topic

Vocabulary

1 Match the pictures with the words below. Write the correct number next to the words.

- [2] argue
- [ ] fight
- [ ] hide
- [ ] hit
- [ ] shout

🎧 **Now listen and repeat.**

Recycling

2 Write the plurals of the words.

1 man ___men___
2 woman _____
3 child _____

Exploring the topic

Witness A
I was standing at the bus stop. It was six fifteen and I was waiting for the bus. It was raining. Two men were fighting on the street corner. They were standing by a wrecked car. One man was holding a gun. A woman was hiding around the corner. Another woman was looking inside a big bag on the sidewalk. She was talking on a cell phone.

Witness B
It was six fifteen. I was driving down the street. Two men were standing on the street corner. They were standing by a wrecked car and they were arguing. One man was hitting the other one. There was a big bag on the sidewalk. A woman was looking inside the bag. She was holding a cell phone but she wasn't talking. Another woman was hiding around the corner.

Witness C
I was closing my shop at six fifteen. Two men were arguing on the street corner. They were standing by a wrecked car. They were shouting. One of them was holding a knife. A young woman was looking inside a bag on the sidewalk. The woman was talking on her cell phone. There was a gun next to the bag. Another woman was hiding around the corner.

Reading

1 Look at the picture. Find:
1 a gun   2 a knife   3 a bus stop
4 a sidewalk   5 a wrecked car

2 🎧 Read and listen to the witness statements. Which one matches the picture exactly?

Grammar
Past progressive (affirmative / negative)
Talking about actions in progress in the past

1 Look at the chart.

Affirmative	Negative
I **was** arguing.	I **wasn't** fighting.
You **were** running.	You **weren't** walking.
He / She / It **was** hiding.	He / She / It **wasn't** shouting.
We / You / They **were** talking.	We / You / They **weren't** hiding.

2 Circle the correct form.

It was four o'clock yesterday afternoon. The sun (1) **wasn't** / weren't shining. It (2) was / were raining. Daisy and Kit (3) was / were waiting for the bus. They (4) was / were standing inside the bus shelter because the wind (5) was / were blowing and the girls (6) weren't / wasn't carrying umbrellas.

3 What were the people doing or not doing at 6 p.m. yesterday? Use the words in parentheses.

1 The young woman ___wasn't dancing___ (dance).

2 The two boys _____. (play a video game)

3 The two girls _____. (sing)

4 The old man _____. (eat)

5 The young man _____. (work on the computer)

6 The old woman _____. (cry)

4 Complete the dialog. Use the correct form of the verbs in parentheses.

Teacher: What was the problem during study period, boys?

Peter: Tom (1) ___was talking___. (talk)

Tom: That isn't true! I (2) _____. (not talk) I (3) _____ (read) my book.

Peter: You (4) _____! (not read) Your book wasn't open!

Tom: Well, you (5) _____ (send) a text message. I saw you!

Peter: I (6) _____ (not send) a text message! My phone was in my bag.

Teacher: Well, boys, I (7) _____ (not watch) so I don't know what happened. Let's just forget it, okay?

Finished?
Page 109, Puzzle 7A

Over to you!

5 Write two true and one false sentence about yesterday. Use the affirmative and negative past progressive. Can the class guess which sentence is false?

Student A: 1 At six p.m. yesterday I was doing my homework.
2 I wasn't having dinner at eight o'clock.
3 I was watching TV at eight thirty.
Student B: Sentence 2 is false.
Student A: No, it's true.
Student B: Sentence 3 is false.
Student A: Yes, it's false. I was reading at eight thirty.

59

Building the topic

2 On April 6th, at 4:50 p.m. they were at Ellen's _____.

3 On April 8th, at 6:10 p.m. Ellen was on the _____.

1 On April 6th, at 3:50 p.m. Jason and Mark were at the ____bank____.

APRIL 8
6:10 P.M.

APRIL 6
3:50 P.M.

5 On April 8th, at 6:15 p.m. they were arguing on the _____.

4 On April 8th, at 6:10 p.m. Jason and Mark were in the _____.

APRIL 8
6:15 P.M.

APRIL 8
6:10 P.M.

Vocabulary

1 Look at the pictures. Fill in the blanks with the words below.

> apartment   garage   police station
> fire escape   street corner   bank

🎧 Now listen and repeat.

6 On April 8th, at 6:50 p.m. Jason, Mark and Ellen were at the _____.

APRIL 8
6:50 P.M.

2 🎧 Read and listen to the interviews with the suspects. Two people are telling the truth. Who are they?

Ellen Richards
Police: What were you doing on the fire escape at six ten p.m.?
Ellen: I was taking the money to Mark and Jason. Mark is my boyfriend.

Jason Duvall
Police: Why were you arguing with Mark Harris on the street corner at six fifteen p.m.?
Jason: He was angry because I crashed his car.
Police: Were you going to get the money from Ellen Richards?
Jason: Yes, we were. She was carrying it down the fire escape.

Mark Harris
Police: Why were you arguing with Jason Duvall at six fifteen p.m.?
Mark: I was angry because he crashed my car.
Police: Were you going to get the money from Ellen Richards?
Mark: I don't know Ellen Richards.

3 Circle T (True) or F (False).

1 Mark and Jason were robbing the bank at 3:50 p.m. on April 6th.   Ⓣ/ F

2 On April 6th, at 4:50 p.m., they were at Jason's apartment.   T / F

3 Ellen dropped the bag of money by accident.   T / F

4 Jason and Mark were arguing because Mark crashed Jason's car.   T / F

5 Jason and Mark were going to get the money from Ellen.   T / F

Grammar
Past progressive (questions)
Asking about actions in progress in the past

1 Look at the chart.

yes / no questions	Answers
Was I runn**ing**?	Yes, I **was**. / No, I **wasn't**.
Were you hid**ing**?	Yes, you **were**. / No, you **weren't**.
Was he / she / it argu**ing**?	Yes, he / she / it **was**. No, he / she / it **wasn't**.
Were we / you / they fight**ing**?	Yes, we / you / they **were**. No, we / you / they **weren't**.

wh- questions	
Where were you go**ing**?	I was going to the movies.
What were you do**ing** at 9 p.m.?	I was doing my homework.

2 Put the words in order to make questions.

1 were / what / you / at / doing / seven p.m.?
   _What were you doing at seven p.m._____ ?

2 to / was / he / talking / Marcy / last night?
   _____ ?

3 they / what / watching / yesterday afternoon / were / on TV?
   _____ ?

4 yesterday morning / was / she / where / going?
   _____ ?

5 they / why / running / were?
   _____ ?

6 he / last week / arguing / was / with Fran?
   _____ ?

3 Match the answers with the questions from exercise 2.

1 They were watching a show about ancient history. _3_

2 Yes, he was. He was asking her about her holiday. ____

3 I was playing soccer at seven p.m. ____

4 Because they were afraid. ____

5 Yes, he was. They were arguing about a girl. ____

6 She was going to the library. ____

4 Write questions. Use the underlined part of the answers to help you.

1 _What were you looking for_____ ?
   I was looking for my history book.

2 _____ ?
   Tyler was running because he was late.

3 _____ ?
   They were waiting for us outside the mall.

4 _____ ?
   He was watching the evening news.

5 _____ ?
   I was going to the movies.

6 _____ ?
   I was having lunch at twelve o'clock yesterday.

Finished?
Page 109, Puzzle 7B

Over to you!

5 Look at the strange activities below. Ask and answer in class about why you were doing these activities. Think of a good answer!

wear a clown costume   climb on the roof
read in the shower   sing in the street
dance in your classroom   carry a monkey

Student A: Why were you wearing a clown costume yesterday?
Student B: Because I was going to a party.
Student A: Good. Your turn.
Student B: Why were you … ?

Living English

DUMB CRIMINALS

Criminals aren't always the smartest people in the world. Here are some of the funniest examples.

1 A burglar was stealing a computer. He didn't know that the webcam was running, and the camera was sending a recording to the owner of the computer. The owner called the police and they caught the burglar!

2 A man was traveling along a freeway in Colorado. He was driving in a special fast lane. It was for cars with two or more passengers. A police car was driving next to him. The police officer saw that the passenger in the man's car wasn't moving. In fact, the passenger wasn't real. The man was riding with a dummy! The police fined him $115.

3 Two men stole a car from a gas station. The owner of the car was working in the station. She called the police. About an hour later she was cleaning the parking area. A car stopped at the station – her car! The car needed gas, so the thieves decided to come back and fill up. What were they thinking?

4 A man and his girlfriend were robbing a convenience store. The man was collecting the money, and the woman was waiting for him. Then the girlfriend saw an advertisement for a contest. The prizes were really cool, so she filled out the form with her name, address and phone number. The police arrested the couple a few hours later at their house.

Reading 🎧

Before you read

1 Look at the pictures and read the title and subtitle. What is the text about?

a   stupid police officers?

b   stupid criminals?

While you read

2 Read the article. What were the criminals doing? Write the number of the story.

1   stealing from a store   _4_

2   stealing from a home   ____

3   breaking a traffic law   ____

4   stealing a car   ____

After you read

3 Read the article again. Circle T (True) or F (False).

1   The owner of the computer knew that the burglar was stealing it.   (T)/ F

2   Two people were sitting in the car in Colorado when the police stopped him.   T / F

3   The car thieves came back to return the woman's car. T / F   T / F

4   The police easily found out the home address of the convenience store robbers.   T / F

Listening 🎧

1 Look at the Listening skills box.

Listening skills

Predicting vocabulary

Before you listen you can predict the words you're going to hear.

Now look at the pictures. Who says the words below? Write G (Gwen) or M (Maria).

1 shouting ____   4 running ____

2 books ____   5 earthquake ____

3 car ____

Listen and check.

Gwen

Maria

2 Listen to the conversation again. Circle the correct answer.

1 Gwen was sleeping / reading last night.

2 Gwen was shouting / laughing.

3 Gwen was scared / not scared.

4 Maria was driving / working last night.

5 Maria saw cars crashing / people running.

Speaking 🎧

1 Listen and read.

Hey, Chester. What were you doing yesterday afternoon?

I was running a marathon.

No way!

Well, I was really running around the park.

Hi, Alex. What were you doing yesterday afternoon?

I was recording a song for my CD.

You're kidding!

Yes, I am. I was doing my homework.

2 Look at the Pronunciation box. Listen to the examples.

Pronunciation

Expressing surprise

We express surprise with our intonation.
No way!
You're kidding!

Listen again and repeat.

3 Listen. Put ✓ (expresses surprise) or ✗ (doesn't express surprise).

1 That's boring. _✗_

2 You're kidding. ____

3 That's amazing. ____

4 That's interesting. ____

5 No way! ____

4 Practice the dialog with your partner.

5 Change the words in blue. Write a new dialog. Now practice the dialog in class.

Review 7

Vocabulary

Verbs

1 Fill in the blanks with the correct form of the words below. Use the *-ing* form where necessary.

> argue hit fighting hiding shout

1 Don't ___argue___ with me. You know I'm right.
2 Don't _____ your brother.
3 "Where's José? I can't find him."
  "He's _____."
4 You don't have to _____. I can hear you.
5 Ted and Gavin are _____ because Ted broke Gavin's computer.

Places

2 Match the sentences 1–6 with the places A–F.

1 "Where's the store?"
2 "The building is on fire!"
3 "Where's the car? I can't find it."
4 "You're under arrest."
5 "Can I open an account, please?"
6 "It's on the fifth floor."

A bank
B apartment
C police station
D fire escape
E garage
F street corner

Grammar

Past progressive (affirmative / negative)

1 Look at the picture. Write sentences about Mariel and Josh. Use the words in parentheses in the past progressive affirmative or negative.

7 o'clock

1 _They weren't running_ . (they / run)
2 _____. (Josh / look at a map)
3 _____. (Mariel / drive)
4 _____. (Josh / talk on the phone)
5 _____. (Mariel / shout)
6 _____. (they / laugh)

Past progressive (questions)

2 Write questions for the answers.

Ali: (1) _What were you doing_ at seven o'clock yesterday?
Mariel: I was driving at seven o'clock yesterday.
Ali: (2) _____?
Mariel: I was going to Jacksonville.
Ali: (3) _____?
Mariel: I was going there because I wanted to visit my parents.
Ali: (4) _____?
Mariel: Yes, Josh was going with me.
Ali: (5) _____?
Mariel: Yes, we were arguing.
Ali: (6) _____?
Mariel: We were arguing because we were lost!

Study skills

Using a dictionary

A dictionary can help you to understand new vocabulary. A monolingual English dictionary gives an explanation in English, and some more information.

1 Look at the dictionary entry for *argue*.

① ② ③ ④

★**argue** /ˈɑrgyu/ *verb* **1** [I] **argue (with sb) (about/over sth)** to say things (often angrily) that show that you do not agree with sb about sth: *The people next door are always arguing. I never argue with my husband about money.*

⑤ ⑥

Match the numbers with the information.

Spelling _1_   Example ____
Pronunciation ____   Stress ____
Definition / meaning ____   Part of speech ____

8 Survivors

Grammar: past progressive and simple past; adverbs of manner
Vocabulary: natural disasters; adverbs of manner

Introducing the topic

Vocabulary

1 Match the photos with the words below. Write the correct number next to the words.

5 blizzard	earthquake	tornado	
hurricane	tsunami	hailstorm	
flood	forest fire		

🎧 **Now listen and repeat.**

Recycling

2 Put the words from exercise 1 in the correct column.

fire	wind	water	earth
	tornado		

65

Exploring the topic

THE DAY AFTER TOMORROW

Background

At the start of the film, people all over the world were living their normal lives. But at the same time, the weather was becoming more and more extreme. Temperatures were going up, and the sea was getting colder and colder. World leaders were meeting to talk about changes in the weather. Scientists were studying the effects of the change.

Jack Hall was a scientist from Washington. He was studying weather changes in Antarctica.

The story

Jack predicted a new Ice Age but nobody believed him. Suddenly, disasters started to happen all over the world. Hurricanes destroyed Hawaii. Tornadoes hit Los Angeles. A tsunami flooded New York. The Statue of Liberty disappeared under the water. Hailstorms hit Tokyo, and blizzards destroyed New Delhi, in India. The polar ice caps melted and temperatures fell. The Ice Age began.

Jack decided to save his teenage son, Sam, who was on vacation in New York. He started his journey with a couple of friends. Jack and his friends walked for days in the snow and strong winds. They survived many disasters and finally met Sam. He was in the New York Library with some other survivors.

The end

At the end of the film, there was hope for the survivors. The sun was shining, and life was starting again.

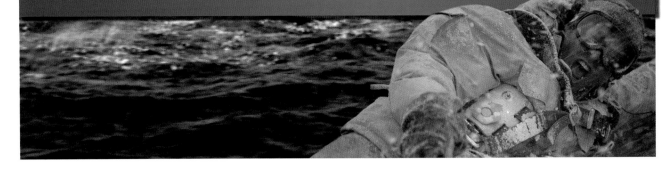

Reading

1 Read the text and put the sentences in order.

The sun came out and the weather changed again. ____

Natural disasters were happening all over the World. ____

Scientist Jack predicted a new Ice Age. ____

Scientists and word leaders were discussing the weather changes. _1_

Jack started a long journey to save his son. ____

2 Read and listen to the text. Fill in the blanks with the words below.

| a tsunami | blizzards | tornadoes | hailstorms |
| hurricanes |

1 _A tsunami_ flooded New York.

2 _____ destroyed Hawaii.

3 _____ destroyed New Delhi.

4 _____ hit Tokyo.

5 _____ hit Los Angeles.

Grammar
Past progressive and simple past
Talking about actions in progress and completed actions in the past

1 Look at the chart.

Action in progress	Completed action
He **was studying** climate change.	A tornado **hit** New York.
They **weren't having** dinner.	We **didn't go** out last night.

2 Match the action in progress, 1–6 with the completed action, A–F.

Action in progress

1 Helen was swimming.
2 Mark was climbing a snowy mountain.
3 Lara and John were watching TV.
4 Julia was cleaning her room.
5 Carlos was having a bad dream.
6 Helen and Jim were camping.

Completed actions

A He cried and fell out of bed.
B They heard a noise and went downstairs.
C She saw a shark and got out of the water.
D They saw a lion near the tent and ran away.
E He slipped on the ice and broke his leg.
F She found an old diary and showed it to her mom.

3 Fill in the blanks with the past progressive of the verbs in parentheses.

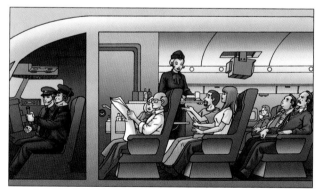

I'm a pilot and this is what happened on my last trip.
We (1) _were flying_ (fly) the plane and everything
(2) _____ (work) well. My co-pilot, Jack and I
(3) _____ (check) the plane controls, the flight
attendants (4) _____ (serve) dinner and most
of the passengers (5) _____ (watch) a movie.
A few people (6) _____ (read).

4 Now finish the story. Fill in the blanks with the simple past of the verbs in parentheses.

Half an hour later, the plane (1) _started_ (start) to
go down, the temperature (2) _____ (go) up.
Jack (3) _____ (look) at me. We didn't know
what was wrong.
I (4) _____ (call) the control tower but the
people (5) _____ (not answer). We were very
worried. After a few minutes a strong wind
(6) _____ (hit) the plane and the plane went
up again.

Finished?
Page 109, Puzzle 8A

Over to you!

5 **Tell your friend about a good / bad dream.
What was happening in your dream?**

Student A: I was surfing in Hawaii.
Student B: It was a good dream.
Student A: I was running away from two criminals.
Student B: It was a bad dream.

Building the topic

1 Last year sixteen-year-old Lynsey Walters was traveling happily home on the bus after meeting her friends.

2 There were two boys at the back of the bus. They were annoying two passengers. Lynsey looked at them. They shouted and walked towards her angrily. Lynsey was scared.

3 Another passenger, Mr. Mark McCusker, told them quietly to leave Lynsey alone.

4 The boys started to shout loudly. One of the boys took out a knife and attacked the man.

5 Lynsey didn't stop to think. She ran quickly towards one of the boys, and kicked him hard.

6 Mr. McCusker's injuries were very bad! Lynsey tried to keep him awake. The bus driver drove carefully to the hospital.

7 Lynsey later got an award for her act of bravery. She was the youngest person on the bus but she took action and controlled the situation very well.
Mr. McCusker only survived thanks to her.

Brave Ly

Walters accepts a medal for bravery.

Vocabulary

1 Match the pictures with the words below. Write the correct number next to the words.

2 angrily	quietly	loudly
well	carefully	hard
quickly	happily	

🎧 Listen and repeat.

2 🎧 Read and listen to the text. Circle T (True) or F (False).

1 Lynsey was traveling to school.   T / F

2 There were three boys at the back of the bus.   T / F

3 One of the boys had a knife.   T / F

4 Mr. McCusker kicked one of the boys.   T / F

5 Lynsey got an award for saving Mr. McCusker.   T / F

Grammar

Adverbs of manner

Talking about how we do things

1 Look at the chart.

Regular adverbs		
Adjective	**Adverb**	**Example**
quiet	quiet**ly**	She was talking **quietly**.
happy	happ**ily**	The girl was smiling **happily**.
easy	eas**ily**	He did the exam **easily**.

Irregular adverbs		
good	**well**	She plays tennis **well**.
hard	**hard**	She was working **hard**.
fast	**fast**	She ran **fast**.

2 Change the adjectives to adverbs.

1 Jack is a careful driver. He drives _carefully_ .

2 Mary is a happy teacher. She teaches _____.

3 Jack is a good climber. He climbs _____.

4 Alex is a fast driver. He drives _____.

5 Mary and Tom are angry neighbors. They talk _____.

6 Jack is a hard worker. He works _____.

3 Fill in the blanks with the adverbs of the adjectives below.

bad   fast   angry   good   hard   loud

1 Andy kicked the ball _hard_ .

2 Vanessa was singing _____.

3 Andrea was running _____.

4 Phil was playing the guitar _____.

5 Laura was dancing _____.

6 They were shouting _____.

Take note!

Adjectives describe nouns.

Bob is a **quiet** boy.

Adverbs decribe verbs.

He opened the door **quietly**.

4 Circle the adjective or adverb.

I walked (1) slow / (slowly) to the bus stop. It was a (2) beautiful / beautifully day. At the bus stop I met a (3) happy / happily girl. She talked (4) kind / kindly to me. She was a (5) brave / bravely explorer from Austria. She talked (6) slow / slowly because her English wasn't very (7) good / well. The bus didn't stop, so we waited (8) patient / patiently for the next bus.

Finished?
Page 109, Puzzle 8B

Over to you!

5 Say four things you did. Can the class guess HOW you did them?

Student A: I played tennis.
Student B: You played badly.
Student A: No. I played well. I climbed a mountain.
Student B: You climbed fast.
Student A: Yes, you're right.

Living English

Surviving the storm
- a true story

In 1985, Joe Simpson and Simon Yates started their dangerous climb up Siula Grande, a very tall mountain in Peru. After three days they reached the top, but they didn't have much food left. They needed to go down quickly!

Then disaster happened! Simpson fell and broke his leg. The two men tied themselves together with a long rope, and continued down the mountain, very slowly. But that wasn't the end of their problems. During a snowstorm, Simpson fell off the edge of the mountain. He was hanging from the rope, and Yates was starting to fall too! They shouted but they didn't hear or see each other. Yates held the rope for an hour, but then he had to make a very difficult decision. He didn't want to die, and he thought that his friend was dead. He cut the rope and continued down the mountain alone.

Simpson wasn't dead. He fell 30 meters and landed in an ice cave. It was cold and dark. He didn't have any food or water, and he had a broken leg. He desperately wanted to live! He climbed out of the cave and very slowly began to crawl down the mountain. Finally, three days later, he reached the camp. Simpson and Yates were both safe!

Simpson wrote a book called *Touching the Void* about his experience. In 2003, a movie about this amazing story of survival won awards in the U.K. and the U.S.

Reading

Before you read

1 **What do you think helps people survive? Put these things in order of importance from 1–4.**

Tools ____   Personality ____

Knowledge / Experience ____   Luck ____

While you read

2 **Read the story. Put the events in order.**

Simpson fell and broke his leg. ____

Yates and Simpson climbed Siula Grande. _1_

A snowstorm hit the mountain. ____

Both climbers survived. ____

Yates and Simpson went down tied together with a rope. ____

After you read

3 **Fill in the blanks in the newspaper report with the words below.**

snowstorm   survived   ice   rope   book
leg   cut   Siula Grande

Simon Yates and Joe Simpson climbed (1) _Siula Grande_ , in Peru. When they were coming down, Simpson fell and broke his (2) _____. Simpson and Yates used a (3) _____ to go down. Later, a (4) _____ hit the mountain. Yates had to (5) _____ the rope. Simpson fell on (6) _____. Both men (7) _____. Later, Simpson wrote a (8) _____.

Listening 🎧

1 Look at the photos. Do you know David Coulthard? What's his job?

David Coulthard

2 Listen and choose A or B.

The survival story is about:
A   A racing driver's plane accident in France.
B   A racing driver's car accident in France.

3 Listen again. Fill in the blanks with the words below.

> France   went to the hospital
> made an emergency call   private jet
> caught fire   his girlfriend

1   David Coulthard was flying to _France_ .
2   He was traveling in his _____.
3   He was traveling with _____.
4   The plane had a problem, so the pilot _____.
5   The pilot was landing and the plane _____.
6   David and his girlfriend escaped and _____.

Writing

1 Look at the Writing skills box.

Writing skills

first, then, next and *finally*

We use *first, then, next* and *finally* to sequence events.
First, I called my friend. Then, we went to the movies.
Next, we had a pizza and finally, I went home.

2 Now read the text. Put the paragraphs in order.

____ First, a big storm hit Ray's neighborhood. Then, the ground opened and aliens appeared. The aliens destroyed humans and cities.

____ Finally, Ray caused an explosion and destroyed the aliens. The family escaped and arrived safely in Boston.

____ Next, Ray decided to take his children back to Boston quickly. But a group of aliens caught Ray and Rachel.

_1_ Ray Ferrier (Tom Cruise) lived in New Jersey. His son, Robbie and daughter, Rachel traveled from Boston to spend the weekend with him. But a disaster changed their plans and their lives.

3 Fill in the chart with information about *War of the Worlds*.

	War of the Worlds
Characters and place	Ray: _father (Tom Cruise)_
	Rachel: _____
	Robbie: _____
	Place: _____
What happened	First: _____
	Then: _____
	Next: _____
The End	Finally: _____

4 Now make notes about a movie that you like.

5 Write about the movie in exercise 4. Use the text and your notes to help you.

Review 8

Vocabulary
Natural disasters

1 Unscramble the words below.

1 tandoor _tornado_
2 zabdrli _____
3 uarhecinr _____
4 rotsef reif _____
5 mnsuiat _____
6 olofd _____
7 ktraeuahqe _____
8 mrlhtiosa _____

Adverbs of manner

2 Fill in the blanks with the adverbs of the adjectives below.

> angry   good   fast   quiet   hard

1 Lisa was running __fast__ because she was late.
2 Dave broke a glass, and his mom shouted _____.
3 You have to speak _____ in the library.
4 My soccer team won all their games last year. They played very _____.
5 I studied _____ and passed the exam.

Grammar
Past progressive and simple past

1 Fill in the blanks with the past progressive form of the verbs in parentheses.

I (1) _was walking_ (walk) along the beach with a friend. The sun (2) _____ (shine), and the birds (3) _____ (sing).
Some young people (4) _____ (play) volleyball. Some older people (5) _____ (play) cards. A teenage girl (6) _____ (listen) to music. But …

2 Now finish the story. Fill in the blanks with the simple past form of the verbs in parentheses.

But soon a strong wind (1) _hit_ (hit) the coast and it (2) _started_ (start) to rain. The birds (3) _____ (fly) away, the young people (4) _____ (run) to their cars and (5) _____ (drive) home.
We (6) _____ (go) to the café near the beach and (7) _____ (have) a cup of coffee. We (8) _____ (wait) for the storm to finish.

Adverbs of manner

3 Fill in the blanks with the adverbs of the adjectives in parentheses.

1 I shouted _loudly_ (loud) but my mom didn't hear me.
2 He's smiling _____ (happy) because he's passed the exam.
3 My dad always drives very _____ (careful).
4 They climbed the mountain _____ (easy).
5 Our team played _____ (good) but we lost the game.
6 It was raining _____ (hard) when we left the house.

Reading

A true story

On Christmas Eve, 1971, German teenager Juliane Koepcke took a flight from Lima to meet her father in Pucallpa. But the plane never arrived. When the plane was going through a storm the 17-year-old girl looked out the window. She saw that the wing was on fire. And that was the last thing Juliane remembered.

She woke up three hours later, in the jungle. She had some broken bones but she was alive. She looked around but found only some empty seats and parts of the plane. Of the 92 people on the plane, Juliane was the only survivor.

Then, she remembered her father's advice: "Follow the river to find civilization". Juliane walked along the river. Sometimes she heard planes, but they didn't see her.

On the tenth day, she found a house, and rested for a while. The next day, a group of Peruvian hunters arrived at the house. They took her to the town of Tournavista, and a local pilot flew Juliane to her father, in Pucallpa.

1 Circle T (True) or F (False).

1 Juliane was going to meet her father.   (T)/ F
2 A hurricane hit the plane.   T / F
3 Juliane woke up in the desert.   T / F
4 All the 92 people on the plane survived.   T / F
5 Juiliane followed the river.   T / F
6 Peruvian hunters found Juliane.   T / F

Grammar: *should / shouldn't; going to*
Vocabulary: *exercise verbs; sports*

Introducing the topic

1 *kick*

2

3

4

5

6

7

8

Recycling

2 Label the parts of the body.

1
2
3
4
5
6

1 Label the pictures with the words below.

| stretch | bend | kick | spin | jump | hit |
| pass | land | | | | |

🎧 **Now listen and repeat.**

Exploring the topic

Reading

1 Read the text once. *Sepak takraw* is a mixture of three sports. What are they?

UNUSUAL SPORTS

Sepak takraw

This is one of the most amazing sports in the world, and one of the most exciting. The game is originally from Indonesia. Imagine gymnastics, soccer and volleyball all in one game.

Equipment
The *takraw* ball is made of rattan (a kind of plant) or hard plastic and weighs about 250 grams. The net is just like a volleyball net.
You should wear comfortable shoes and you shouldn't wear loose or long shorts because you have to kick high and move your legs a lot.

Getting ready
This game is hard work. You should always warm up and stretch before playing. You should also practice jumping and bending your knees when you land.

Playing
There are three players on each team.
You have to hit the ball over the net. You can use your legs, back, head or feet. You win points when the ball touches the floor on the other side.
For soccer players, the basic moves are natural: kicking the ball, hitting it with your head and moving it with your body.

But there are some very complicated moves, for example, jumping high and spinning like a helicopter. New players shouldn't try these tricks. You should have some gymnastics lessons first.
One question people often ask is: Should young children play this game? The answer is: Yes, BUT they shouldn't hit the ball with their heads.

SO... learn, practice and enjoy!

2 🎧 Read and listen to the text. Fill in the blanks with the correct word.

1 Sepak takraw is from _Indonesia_ .

2 There are _____ players on a team.

3 You shouldn't wear loose or long _____.

4 You should _____ before you play.

5 If you want to do complicated moves, you should have some _____ lessons.

6 Young children shouldn't hit the ball with their _____ .

Grammar

should / shouldn't

Giving advice

1 Look at the chart.

Affirmative	Negative
You **should** warm up.	You **shouldn't** wear long shorts.

Questions	Answers
Should I exercise more?	Yes, you **should**. / No, you **shouldn't**.
What **should** I do?	You **should** have a lesson.

2 Look at the pictures. Circle *should* or *shouldn't*.

Advice for baseball

1 You should / shouldn't warm up before you play baseball.

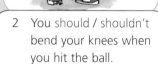

2 You should / shouldn't bend your knees when you hit the ball.

3 You should / shouldn't practice batting every day.

4 You should / shouldn't watch the ball carefully.

5 You should / shouldn't hold the bat low.

6 You should / shouldn't wear a helmet when you are batting.

3 Put the words in order to make sentences about studying.

1 sit / should / at a desk / you
   You should sit at a desk .

2 should / take / you / regular breaks
   _____ .

3 study / shouldn't / you / for a long time
   _____ .

4 a good light / should / use / you
   _____ .

5 shouldn't / watch TV / you
   _____ .

6 lie down / you / shouldn't
   _____ .

4 Write questions using *should* and the words in parentheses.

1 A: I don't like hot weather. *When should I go*
      to India? (when / go)
   B: You should go between November and February.

2 A: My next vacation is to New Zealand.
      _____ there? (what / do)
   B: You should go hiking.

3 A: I want to learn to swim.
      _____ ? (I / take lessons)
   B: Yes, you should. You can't learn alone.

4 A: My friend and I can't remember irregular verbs.
      _____ ? (we / study together)
   B: Yes, you should. You can test each other.

5 A: I want to learn to swim.
      _____ ? (where / go)
   B: You should go to your neighborhood sports center.

Finished?
Page 109, Puzzle 9A

Over to you!

5

Write 3 suggestions for a poster called "How to be good at sports." Make a poster to put up in your classroom.

You should practice every day.
You shouldn't practice if you are injured.

Building the topic

I have a great new bicycle, so I'm going to go cycling this summer.
Kathy, 18

We're going to do karate. It's a really cool sport!
Kyle and Tyler, 13 and 15

I'm going to play golf with my grandfather. He's really good, and I want to learn.
Amelia, 15

I'm going to go horseback riding. My horse needs exercise, and so do I.
Josh, 17

I'm going to go water-skiing this summer. I like water and I like going fast!
Benny, 14

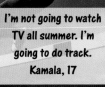

I'm not going to watch TV all summer. I'm going to do track.
Kamala, 17

SUMMER SPORTS RESOLUTIONS

I'm going to play basketball every day. I really want to get better at it.
Geraldo, 15

I'm going to play lacrosse. My friends are going to teach me.
Kelly, 14

Vocabulary

1 Match the photos with the words below. Write the correct number next to the words.

- [2] do karate
- [ ] do track
- [ ] play golf
- [ ] go horseback riding
- [ ] play lacrosse
- [ ] go water-skiing
- [ ] play basketball
- [ ] go cycling

🎧 Now listen and repeat.

2 🎧 Read and listen to the text. Write the names of the people next to the sentences.

1 He's going to do a water sport. __Benny__
2 They're going to use something they already have. _____ and _____
3 He wants to get better at a sport. _____
4 They're going to do a martial art. _____ and _____
5 She's going to learn something from an older person. _____
6 She's not going to watch TV. _____
7 She's going to learn something from her friends. _____

Grammar

going to

Talking about plans and resolutions

1 Look at the chart.

Affirmative	Negative
We're **going to** play tennis.	We are**n't going to** do karate.
She's **going to** do track.	She is**n't going to** go cycling.

Questions	Answers
Are we **going to** exercise every day?	Yes, we **are**. / No. we **aren't**.
What are you **going to** do?	I'm **going to** play lacrosse.

2 Choose the correct form.

1 I'm going _to play_ hockey tomorrow afternoon.
   a play   (b) to play   c playing

2 _____ you going to go skiing this weekend?
   a Do   b Are   c Is

3 Terry _____ going to come to the movies with us.
   a isn't   b doesn't   c won't

4 _____ Luisa going to help us with the project?
   a Are   b Does   c Is

5 We _____ play hockey this weekend.
   a going to   b go to   c are going to

3 Look at Kirsten's list of activities. Write sentences about what she's going to do (✓) and isn't going to do (✗).

Activity Camp

These are some of the activities we offer:

go climbing ✓
do painting and drawing ✗
take music classes ✓
learn to play tennis ✗
go canoeing ✗
work on our magazine ✓

1 _____She's going to_____ go climbing.
2 _____ do painting and drawing.
3 _____ take music classes.
4 _____ learn to play tennis.
5 _____ go canoeing.
6 _____ work on the magazine.

4 Complete the questions. Use the words in parentheses.

A: (1) _What are you going to do_ this summer? (what / you / do)

B: We're going to visit my grandparents in England.

A: (2) _____ them? (why / you / visit)

B: Because we don't see them very often. I miss them.

A: (3) _____? (how long / you / stay)

B: We're going to stay for two months.

A: Wow! (4) _____? (you / visit / London)

B: I'm not sure.

A: (5) _____ here next summer? (your grandparents / come)

B: I don't know. They usually come every two years.

Finished?
Page 109, Puzzle 9B

Over to you!

5 Write sentences with *I'm going to …* and *I'm not going to …* about next weekend. Ask and answer in class.

Student A: What are you going to do this weekend?
Student B: I'm going to play soccer.
Student A: Me too! / I'm not. I'm going to play basketball.

Living English

KUNG FU DREAMS

Reading

Before you read

1 Look at the pictures and the title of the article. What sport does Alex do?

1 Alex Bennett is thirteen years old. He lives in Vancouver, in Washington and he does kung fu. He is one of the best of the 300 students in his
5 school. He started when he was eight years old and he practices four times a week.

Alex would like to be a kung fu teacher, a competitor or an actor
10 in movies. "Movies are exciting," he says, "but the kung fu isn't real. The actors are good and they get a lot of money!"

Of course money isn't the real reason
15 for doing a sport like kung fu. "You shouldn't think too much about being famous or rich," Alex says. "It's more important to think about getting better. Kung fu isn't just a sport –
20 it's a lot more than that."

What advice does Alex have for young people who want to be successful in a sport?
– Be positive. You shouldn't think
25 that everyone is better than you. It isn't true.
– Do other kinds of physical exercise. Your muscles need a change, and your mind does too.
30 – You shouldn't eat too much junk food. Your body works better with good food in it.
– Do well in school. Good grades will keep you on the team, and
35 they will make you feel good too. AND your parents will be happy!
– You should always have goals. They are important to keep you going.

So what are Alex's goals?
40 – I'm going to be a Black Belt in two years.
– I'm not going to use drugs or alcohol.
– I'm going to do better in school.
45 – I'm going to spend a month in a martial arts camp next summer.
– I'm not going to quit. Sometimes you get tired or bored, but you have to keep going.
50 We wish Alex good luck for a great future in martial arts.

While you read

2 Look at the Reading skills box.

Reading skills

Subject reference

Very often a text will use a noun once, then use *it* or *they* after that.

Look at these sentences:

John and Tim play tennis. It is their favorite sport.

It in the second sentence refers to *tennis*, not to *John* or *Tim*.

3 Read the text and find these pronouns in the text. What do they refer to?

1 they (line 12) refers to: a actors   b movies
2 it (line 20) refers to: a money   b kung fu
3 it (line 32) refers to: a your body b food
4 they (line 35) refers to: a parents   b grades
5 They (line 37) refers to: a goals   b sports

After you read

4 Read the article again. Fill in the blanks.

1 There are _300_ students in Alex's school.

2 For Alex, getting better at a sport is more important than _____.

3 Alex says it isn't good to eat _____ _____.

4 Getting good grades is important for you and your _____.

5 Alex is going to get his Black Belt in _____ years.

6 He is going to spend a month in a _____ _____ _____ next summer.

Listening 🎧

1 Listen to the interview and look at the pictures. What did Jason do last year? What is he going to do next?

2 Listen to the interview again. Circle the correct words.

1 Last year, Jason traveled across the United States by (bicycle) / car.

2 Jason's next adventure is to sail across the Pacific / Atlantic Ocean.

3 This trip is going to take four months / two months.

4 Jason says you should exercise / rest before you go.

5 He also says you should get a lot of / a little information before you go.

Speaking 🎧

1 Listen and read.

2 Look at the Pronunciation box. Listen to the examples.

Pronunciation

Silent letters

Some words have "silent" letters.

should /ʃəd/   whole /hoʊl/

Listen again and repeat.

3 Listen. Cross out the silent letters.

1 shouldn't   2 answer   3 island   4 walk   5 talk

Now listen and repeat.

4 Practice the dialog with your partner.

5 Change the words in blue. Write a new dialog. Now practice the dialog in class.

Review 9

Vocabulary
Exercise verbs

1 Fill in the blanks in the verbs.

1 b _e_ _n_ _d_   5 l _ _ _
2 p _ _ _   6 s _ _ _ _ _ _
3 j _ _ _   7 s _ _ _
4 k _ _ _   8 h _ _

Sports

2 Put the words in the correct column.

> water-skiing   basketball   horseback riding
> golf   karate   lacrosse   track   cycling

go	play	do

Grammar
should / shouldn't

1 Put the words in order to make sentences or questions.

1 should / listen / you / to your coach
    You should listen to your coach .

2 I / should / before I exercise / warm up
    _____ ?

3 a lot of / fast food / she / eat / shouldn't
    _____ .

4 they / wear / should / a helmet
    _____ .

5 to your party / I / wear / what / should
    _____ ?

6 fight / he / with his teammates / shouldn't
    _____ .

going to

2 Look at Jason's list of resolutions. Write sentences with *is going to* and *isn't going to*.

YES	NO
practice a lot	stay up late
eat healthy food	eat a lot of fast food
listen to the coach	argue with the referee

1   _He is going to practice a lot_ .
2   _____ .
3   _____ .
4   _____ .
5   _____ .
6   _____ .

3 Put the words in order to make questions.

1 going to / are / go to the zoo / they / tomorrow?
    Are they going to go to the zoo tomorrow ?

2 you / do karate / this year / are / going to?
    _____ ?

3 play soccer / he / going to / is / this evening?
    _____ ?

4 go horse riding / when / going to / we / are?
    _____ ?

5 are / they / go on vacation / this summer / where / going to?
    _____ ?

Study skills

Remembering new vocabulary

You should review new words regularly.

1 Look at the advice for remembering new vocabulary.

1 You should make word cards. Put the English word on the front with a picture, and the translation on the back. Review the cards every week.
2 You should work with a friend. Review the new words together.
3 You should label objects in your room.

2 Choose 5 new words from unit 9 that you are going to learn. Write them here:

1 _____   4 _____
2 _____   5 _____
3 _____

The future

Grammar: *will / won't; too / not enough*
Vocabulary: actions; describing places

Introducing the topic

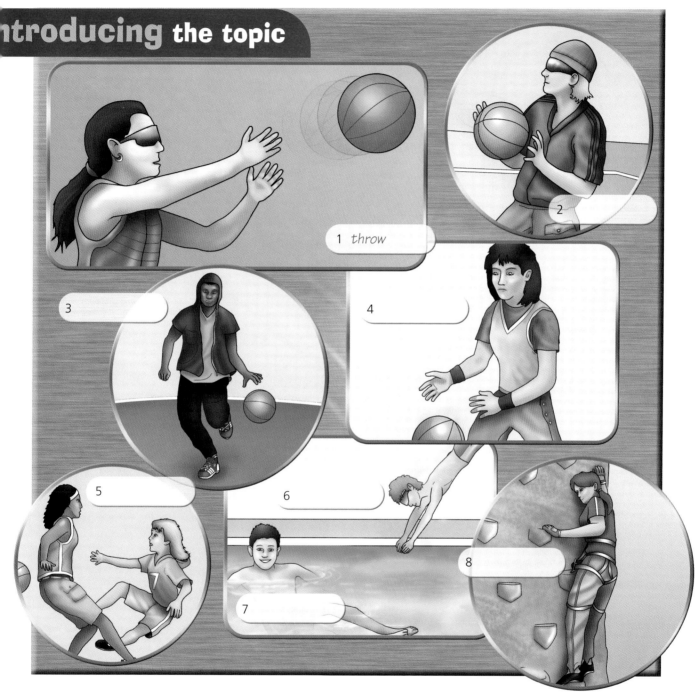

1 throw

Vocabulary

1 Label the photos with the words below.

> climb   bounce   float   dive   bump into
> catch   throw   drop

🎧 Now listen and repeat.

Recycling

2 Match seven of the words from exercise 1 with the nouns below.

Mountain: _climb_

Ball: _____ _____ _____ _____

Swimming pool: _____ _____

Exploring the topic

Space tourism:
Science fiction or science fact?

A What will zero gravity activities be like?

Zero gravity activities will be fun. Imagine ordinary activities like walking. You'll walk slowly and bounce. Then you'll land on your feet like an Olympic gymnast, but slowly.

B How will I have fun in orbit?

There will probably be big playrooms in space hotels. You'll float slowly around, and feel like you're flying. You'll also bump into your friends for fun. You'll drop your drink and catch it in the air.

C Zero gravity water sports

We think hotels will have zero gravity "water rooms". You'll enjoy swimming in a big room full of water with large "water balls" to throw.

D Zero gravity gyms and stadiums

There will probably be zero gravity soccer, rugby and tennis, but with different rules. You'll float in the air!
In gymnasiums you'll jump and make acrobatic movements in the air. You'll also climb and walk on the walls and you won't fall! Remember that the floor and ceiling are the same thing!

E Orbit evenings

In the evenings, after a day full of action, you will feel tired. You'll sit by a big window and watch the blue Earth. You'll see mountains and oceans.

Reading

1 Read the text. Match the idea to the paragraph number.

1 Space tourists will float in the air in big playrooms. _B_

2 Ordinary activities will be fun in orbit. ____

3 People will play sports floating in the air. ____

4 Tourists will watch the Earth through the window. ____

5 People will throw water balls in "water rooms". ____

2 🎧 Read and listen to the text. Circle T (True) or F (False).

1 You'll swim in "water rooms". (T)/ F

2 You'll do martial arts. T / F

3 The rules of zero gravity sports will be different. T / F

4 You'll play soccer in zero gravity stadiums. T / F

5 You'll bump into other planets. T / F

6 You'll catch "water balls" in the air. T / F

Grammar

will / won't

Making predictions about the future

1 Look at the chart.

Affirmative	Negative
I / You / He / She / It **will** travel to space.	I / You / He / She / It **won't** play zero gravity sports.
We / You / They **will** float in space.	We / You / They **won't** travel to space.
There **will be** zero gravity sports.	There **won't be** cars.

2 Put the words in order to make sentences about the future.

1 on vacation / will / People / to space / go
   People will go on vacation to space .

2 under water / people / houses / build / will
   _____ .

3 your house / will / clean / robots
   _____ .

4 won't / there / any pollution / be
   _____ .

5 on the roads / cars / drive / won't
   _____ .

6 be / there / zero gravity soccer / will
   _____ .

3 Look at the chart.

yes / no questions	Answers
Will I / you travel to space?	Yes, I / you **will**. / No, I / you **won't**.
Will he / she / it play zero gravity soccer?	Yes, he / she / it **will**. / No, he / she / it **won't**.
Will we / you / they stay in space hotels?	Yes, we / you / they **will**. / No, we / you / they **won't**.

Wh- questions	Answers
Where will I / you live in ten years' time?	In a big city.
When will he / she / it travel to space?	In 2050.
How will we / you / they travel?	By spaceship.

4 Write the questions about schools in 2050.

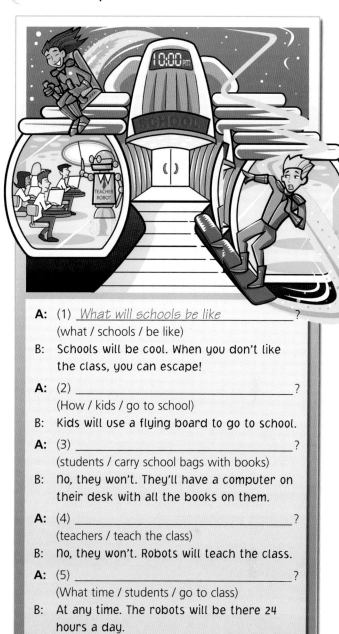

A: (1) *What will schools be like* ?
   (what / schools / be like)
B: Schools will be cool. When you don't like the class, you can escape!

A: (2) _____ ?
   (How / kids / go to school)
B: Kids will use a flying board to go to school.

A: (3) _____ ?
   (students / carry school bags with books)
B: No, they won't. They'll have a computer on their desk with all the books on them.

A: (4) _____ ?
   (teachers / teach the class)
B: No, they won't. Robots will teach the class.

A: (5) _____ ?
   (What time / students / go to class)
B: At any time. The robots will be there 24 hours a day.

Finished?
Page 111, Puzzle 10A

Over to you!

5 Make future predictions about the topics below.

| schools   entertainment   sports   technology |

Student A: We won't go to school. We'll learn at home on the Internet.
Student B: I agree. / I don't agree.

Building the topic

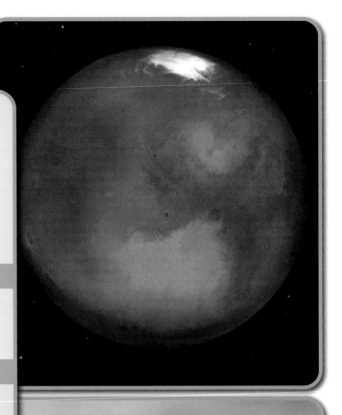

Is life on Mars possible?

Scientists think it'll be possible to send astronauts to Mars in twenty years' time. But will it be possible to live on Mars?

The weather

The weather isn't warm enough and it's too unstable. It can be −133°C in winter!
The planet is icy, and there are dust storms.

The soil

It's too dry. People living on Mars will need food and oxygen, but plants don't grow well.
There isn't any water on the surface.

The atmosphere

It's too dangerous. There isn't any protection from the Sun's dangerous UV rays.
Space radiation can cause health problems.

Distance

It isn't close enough. It takes more than 5 months to travel there.

Vocabulary

1 Read the text. Match the opposites. Use the words below.

> safe   dry   cold   far   stable   warm
> unstable   dangerous   close   wet

1 safe   _dangerous_
2 dry   _____
3 cold   _____
4 far   _____
5 stable   _____

 Now listen and repeat.

2  Read and listen to the text again. Circle T (True) or F (False).

1 Mars is cold.   (T)/ F
2 The weather on Mars isn't stable.   T / F
3 Mars is wet.   T / F
4 The atmosphere is safe.   T / F
5 Mars is far.   T / F

Grammar

too / not enough

Talking about problems

1 Look at the chart.

too + adjective	not + adjective + enough
It's **too** dangerous.	It is**n't** close **enough**.

2 Match sentences 1–5 with sentences A–E.

1 It's too cold.   A It isn't stable enough.

2 Mars is too dry.   B It isn't close enough.

3 It's too dangerous. C It isn't warm enough.

4 It's too unstable.   D It isn't wet enough.

5 It's too far.   E It isn't safe enough.

3 Complete the sentences with *too* and the adjectives below.

> heavy   dry   difficult   expensive   cold

1 The plants don't grow. It's ___too dry___.

2 The cell phone costs $500. It's _____.

3 I can't do this exercise. It's _____.

4 I can't carry the bag. It's _____.

5 I don't like winter. It's _____.

4 Look at the picture. Write sentences with *not enough* and the adjectives in parentheses.

Register for the bike race!

Requirements:
Age: 18–22
Height: 1.75m
Weight: 65–80 kg
Professional bike

1 I want to enter the fun run, but I'm sixteen.
   ___I'm not old enough___. (old)

2 I'm 1.65m tall.
   _____. (tall)

3 I weigh 60 kg.
   _____. (heavy)

4 My bike doesn't work well.
   _____. (safe)

5 My bike is very slow.
   _____. (fast)

5 Look at the pictures. Write sentences with *too* or *not enough*.

1 The car is ___too small___. (small)

2 The beach is _____. (close)

3 Her umbrella is _____. (big)

4 He's _____. (tall)

5 The suitcase is _____. (heavy)

6 The sea is _____. (warm)

Finished?
Page 111, Puzzle 10B

Over to you!

6 Think about an event / concert / party that didn't go well. Why? Tell the class.

Student A: The concert was awful.
Student B: Why?
Student A: The songs were too old. The place wasn't big enough, …

Living English

What do you think will happen to the Earth?

A Some experts say that the Earth's continents will join together to make one big country. Maybe we'll all learn to speak the same language!

Here are some expert theories about the Earth's future.

B "The fish will die and the air and oceans will be polluted," say others. "We will all go to live on other planets."

C In the far distant future, some experts say the Earth's temperature will go up and the oceans will evaporate. The Sun will become hotter and hotter, a big "red giant".

D Other people think the Earth will move away from the Sun and freeze. Who knows – maybe we'll have a new Ice age? Children will ski to school and have polar bears as pets!

E Some optimists are more positive about the Earth's future. They think animals will change and adapt to a new environment. For example, fish will fly and catch food!

Reading 🎧

Before you read

1 What will happen to the Earth in the future? Put ✓ (I agree) or ✗ (I don't agree) next to the sentences. Compare with the class.

1 The sun will get hotter. ____

2 We will have an Ice Age. ____

3 People will live on other planets. ____

While you read

2 Read the article. Write the paragraph letter next to the sentences.

1 We will freeze! _D_

2 Animals will be weird. ____

3 We will live on other planets. ____

4 It's a small world! ____

5 We will fry! ____

After you read

3 Read again. Fill in the blanks with the words below.

> fly   live on other planets   ski   evaporate
> freeze the planet   get hotter   join together

1 The continents will probably _join together_ .

2 The Sun will _____.

3 Fish will _____.

4 The oceans will _____.

5 Children will _____ to school!

6 People will probably _____.

Writing

1 Look at the Writing skills box.

Making predictions

I will live in a big city. (**I'm sure.**)

I'll probably live in a big city. (**I'm not so sure.**)

I don't think I'll live in a big city. (**It's my opinion now but I'm not sure.**)

2 Read the text. Circle two examples of the expressions above in the text.

My future life

I'm Matt Reynolds. I'm 18 years old now. This is how I imagine my life in ten years. I'll live in a small apartment in a big city like New York. The apartment will probably be small and colorful. I'll work for a record company, for example, EMI Records. I'll listen to demos and interview bands. I don't think I'll get married young, but I'll have a girlfriend and go out with friends. I'll also travel to different places, learn about different cultures and meet a lot of people. In my free time, I'll probably go surfing and diving.

3 Fill in the chart with information about Matt's future life.

	Matt's future life
Home	in a big _____
	in a small _____
Work	for a _____ company
Personal life	_____ _____
Free time activities	_____ and _____

4 Now make notes about your future life.

5 Write about your future life. Use the text and your notes to help you.

Speaking

1 Listen and read.

Where will you live in ten years?

I think I'll live in a big city.

I'll probably live here. I like this town.

I'll work for a music magazine.

And you girls? Where will you work in ten years?

I think I'll be a doctor.

And … will you be married?

I don't know. Probably not.

No, but I'm sure I'll have a girlfriend.

2 Look at the Pronunciation box. Listen to the examples.

I and *I'll*

I and **I'll** are different sounds.

I (/aɪ/)	I'll (/aɪl/)
I live in a big city.	I'll live in a big city.
I work for a music magazine.	I'll work for a music magazine.

Listen again and repeat.

3 Listen. Circle the sentence you hear.

1 I play tennis. / I'll play tennis.
2 I work for a record company. / I'll work for a record company.
3 I travel to different places. / I'll travel to different places.

4 Practice the dialog with your partner.

5 Change the words in blue. Write a new dialog. Now practice the dialog in class.

Review 10

Vocabulary
Actions

1 Unscramble the verbs.

1 wrhot _____
2 prod _____
3 eonucb _____
4 iedv _____
5 pbum otin _____
6 olfta _____

Describing places

2 Write the opposites of the words below.

1 safe   _dangerous_
2 close   _____
3 wet   _____
4 stable   _____
5 cold   _____

Grammar
will / won't

1 Read Tammy's predictions about her future. Write sentences with *will* (✓) or *won't* (✗).

My future
live in a big house ✗
work as a singer ✓
live in Australia ✗
have a car ✓
be married ✗
have a boyfriend ✓

1   _She won't live in a big house_ .
2   _____ .
3   _____ .
4   _____ .
5   _____ .
6   _____ .

2 Complete the questions and answers to the questions about Tammy.

1   Will _she live in a big house_ ? _No, she won't_ .
2   Will _____ ? _____ .
3   _____ ? _____ .
4   _____ ? _____ .
5   _____ ? _____ .
6   _____ ? _____ .

too / not enough

3 Fill in the blanks with *too* or *not enough* and the adjectives in parentheses.

1   We can't live on Mars.
It _isn't warm enough_ . (warm)
2   Mary doesn't want to go out at night.
It _____ . (dark)
3   Sheila finishes her homework quickly.
It _____ . (easy)
4   We can't go to Australia on vacation.
It _____ . (close)
5   I can't drink this coffee.
It _____ . (hot)
6   You can't watch the movie.
You _____ . (old)

Reading

1 Read the text. Circle T (True) or F (False).

Megan Lindholm imagines the Earth's future in her story *Alien Earth* (1992). She wants to show the importance of taking care of the environment. These are some of the ideas in her novel.

200 years from now, the planet will be completely destroyed. Friendly aliens will travel to the Earth and take humans to their two planets. On their planets they will teach them how to live in harmony with the environment.

The new generation of humans will live for 200 years. This new kind of humans will not destroy the environment. Picking a flower, or walking on the grass will be crimes. 'Police' aliens will take criminals to a space station. The criminal will stay in prison for the rest of his / her life.

1   The book *Alien Earth* shows that it's   Ⓣ/ F
important to take care of the environment.
2   The story happens 300 years in the future.   T / F
3   The aliens will teach the humans how to   T / F
take care of the environment.
4   The new kind of humans will have a shorter   T / F
life.
5   People who do not take care of the   T / F
environment will go to prison for a long time.

11 Plans

Grammar: present progressive (future plans); *will* (offers)
Vocabulary: TV jobs; health problems

Introducing the topic

Vocabulary

1 Match the photos with the words below. Write the correct number next to the words.

4	acting coach	☐	stylist
☐	makeup artist	☐	dance teacher
☐	bodyguard	☐	hairstylist

🎧 Now listen and repeat.

Recycling

2 Write the correct jobs.

1 act   _actor_____
2 sing   _____
3 model clothes _____
4 dance   _____
5 play soccer _____

Exploring the topic

TOTAL TRANSFORMATION!
The TV show where people change jobs.

Diary of a contestant

My name is Daniel Parker. I'm an electronics engineer. I don't know anything about music – but in one week I'm auditioning to be a singer in a rock group! The group has to believe that I'm a real singer. Crazy? Probably. But I have the chance to win one hundred thousand dollars. And there are a lot of people to help me.
This is the diary of my amazing transformation.

Monday
8 a.m. I'm ready to go! At ten o'clock I'm meeting the team. We're having lunch at two o'clock, and in the evening we're going to a rock concert.

Tuesday
8 a.m. The band last night was fantastic!
This morning at nine I'm meeting the acting coach, the dance teacher and the singing teacher.

10 p.m. Wow! I can really sing! I'm an OK dancer, too. At ten o'clock tomorrow morning I'm meeting the acting coach for some more practice.

Wednesday
10 p.m. Now I can act like a rock star!

Thursday
8 a.m. At ten this morning I'm meeting the fashion team. In the evening I'm performing in front of a thousand people!

midnight That was incredible! Everyone believed I was a singer! Tomorrow is the big day. At ten in the morning I'm practicing with the singing teacher. At two in the afternoon I'm auditioning for the group in the recording studio. I'm really nervous.

Friday
10 p.m. I did it! The group chose me! They thought I was a real rock singer!

Reading

1 **Read the text. Circle T (True) or F (False).**

1 Daniel Parker is a famous rock singer.   T / F

2 *Total Transformation* is a TV show.   T / F

3 Daniel can win some money.   T / F

4 Daniel doesn't have a lot of people to help with his transformation.   T / F

2 🎧 **Read and listen to the text. Fill in Daniel's diary with the words below.**

> 1000   9 a.m.   concert   10 a.m.
> auditioning   acting coach

Monday
(1) _10 a.m._ meeting the team
2 p.m. having lunch
evening going to a (2) _____

Tuesday
(3) _____ meeting the acting coach, dance teacher and singing teacher

Wednesday
10 a.m. meeting the (4) _____

Thursday
10 a.m. meeting the fashion team
8 p.m. performing in front of (5) _____ people!

Friday
2 p.m. (6) _____ for the rock group

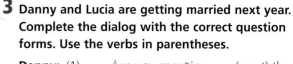

Grammar

Present progressive

Talking about future appointments and arrangements

1 Look at the chart.

Affirmative	Negative
I'm having lunch with Carol at twelve thirty.	I'm not playing tennis tomorrow.

Questions	Answers
Are you **meeting** Maria at eight o'clock?	Yes, **I am**. / No, **I'm not**.
What time **are** you **going** to the movies?	At eight o'clock.

2 Look at Tina's diary. Fill in the blanks with the affirmative or negative form of the present progressive.

1 On Monday morning Tina _is meeting_ managers from AirBorne Shoes. On Monday evening she _____ to a baseball game in Boston.

2 On Tuesday morning she and Kayla _____ to a fashion show. On Tuesday afternoon Tina _____ with a new coach.

3 On Wednesday Tina _____ at a tennis camp. In the evening she and David _____ a movie premiere.

4 On Thursday morning she and Casie _____ to Hawaii on vacation.

Monday
a.m. meeting managers
    from AirBorne Shoes
p.m. going to baseball game
    in Boston cancelled

Tuesday
a.m. going to a fashion
    show with Kayla
p.m. training with new coach

Wednesday
all day: teaching at tennis camp
10 p.m. going to a movie premiere
    with David cancelled

Thursday
a.m. going to Hawaii with Casie on vacation!

3 Danny and Lucia are getting married next year. Complete the dialog with the correct question forms. Use the verbs in parentheses.

Danny: (1) _____Are you meeting_____ (meet) the dress designer tomorrow?

Lucia: Yes, I'm meeting the dress designer at noon. (2) _____ (go) to the travel agent?

Danny: No, I'm not. Your father's doing that. (3) _____ (have) dinner in the evening?

Lucia: Yes, we are. We're eating at Le Lapin.

Danny: (4) What time _____ _____ (eat)?

Lucia: We're eating at seven o'clock.

Danny: (5) _____ (meet) the wedding planner next week?

Lucia: Yes, we're meeting her on Monday.

Danny: Oh no! I'm flying to New York on Monday.

Lucia: (6) _____ _____ (come back)?

Danny: I'm coming back on Thursday. Maybe we can meet her on Friday.

Finished?
Page 111, Puzzle 11A

Over to you!

4 Look at the list of activities. Choose three activities and fill in the diary. Ask and answer in class.

play tennis / soccer / basketball
go to the movies / a party / a concert

Morning
Afternoon
Evening

Student A: Are you playing tennis in the morning?
Student B: No, I'm not.
Student C: Are you meeting your friends in the morning?
Student B: Yes, I am. Are you … ?

Building the topic

Vocabulary

1 Look at the pictures. Fill in the blanks in the speech bubbles with the words below.

> headache   sprained ankle   sore throat
> toothache   pimple   sunburn   blister   cold

🎧 **Now listen and repeat.**

2 Match the offers to the health problems.

a I'll get you a tissue. __4__

b I'll give you my skin lotion. ____

c I'll give you some acne cream. ____

d I'll give you a throat lozenge. ____

e I'll get you an aspirin. ____

f I'll make a dentist appointment for you. ____

g I'll take you to the hospital. ____

h I'll get you a Band-Aid. ____

1 I have a __pimple__!

2 I have a _____!

3 I have a _____!

4 I have a _____!

5 I have a _____!

6 I have a _____!

7 I have a _____!

8 I have a _____!

Grammar

will (offers)

Making offers

1 Look at the chart.

Problem	Offer
I have a headache.	**I'll get** you some aspirin.
I'm hungry.	**I'll make** you a sandwich.

2 Match the problems 1–6 and the offers A–F.

1 You're driving too fast!
2 I'm really bored!
3 The light is too bright!
4 My coffee is cold.
5 I can't understand this exercise.
6 My hair is too long!

A I'll get your sunglasses.
B I'll slow down.
C I'll explain it to you.
D I'll cut it for you.
E I'll get a movie.
F I'll make you another cup.

3 Make offers to the people in the pictures. Use the phrases below.

put a Band-Aid on it   cook the dinner
style it for you   call an ambulance   carry it
show you how to do it

1 *I'll call an*
   ambulance   .

2 _____
   _____ .

3 _____
   _____ .

4 _____
   _____ .

5 _____
   _____ .

6 _____
   _____ .

4 Write offers with the words below.

teach   fix   wash   explain   take

1 A friend is having trouble with his math homework. You are good at math.
   I'll explain it to you   .

2 A friend's bicycle has a flat tire. You are good at fixing things. _____ .

3 You want to help your mom to wash the dishes.
   _____ .

4 A friend doesn't know how to play a game.
   _____ .

5 Your sister needs to get somewhere very quickly. You have a motorcycle.
   _____ .

Finished?
Page 111, Puzzle 11B

Over to you!

5 Tell your problems to the class. Can they make offers?

Student A: I have a broken leg.
Student B: I'll call an ambulance.

Living English

Reading 🎧

Before you read

1 Look at the pictures and the advertisements. Where are the advertisements from?

1 a website   2 a newspaper   3 a magazine

While you read

2 Read the ads again. Write the number of the correct ad next to the statements.

1 It offers services for people who want to get fit. __2__

2 It is for people who want to learn a new skill. ____

3 People with physical problems can call this place. ____

4 It helps you choose what colors to wear. ____

5 It helps you eat healthily. ____

6 You can perform in public with this service. ____

After you read

3 Which service would you like to use? Why / why not?

The Ad Page

① Find the Musician in you!

Are you dreaming of becoming a musician? We'll match you with a teacher who will train, guide and encourage you. We'll give you a program with one-on-one lessons. We'll also arrange for you to play with others and even perform in public!

Perfecta Music Center
tel: 1-606-222-2212
www.yourperfectamusic.eng

Want to be fit and healthy? ②

We'll design a diet and exercise program just for you. We'll provide monthly menus with cooking tips and a personal trainer to help you with your exercise program. All this at a reasonable price, and your satisfaction guaranteed!

OnTrack Nutrition Centers
Call: 1-606-999-1234 for a center near you.

③ Headaches? Backache?

The Massage and Acupuncture Clinic will find the solution to your problems! Our massage therapists and acupuncturists will do tests to identify your problem and will treat you. You'll feel good again! Call for an appointment today!

The MA Clinic
880 Fifth Street West
Selig, California
tel: 101-9962

Color Consultants ④

Do you always wear black because it's the "safest" color? Do you want to find the right colors for you? Color Consultants will look at your hair, eyes and skin and create a Personal Color Profile. We'll even take you shopping and help you find the right clothes and makeup.

We'll bring color to your world!

Call: 1-606-0899-98089
or visit our website:
www.colorconsultants.eng

Listening 🎧

1 Look at the Listening skills box.

2 Listen and circle the correct number.

1   3:15   (3:50)
2   19 West Street   90 West Street
3   January 8th   January 18th
4   1:14   1:40
5   $13.00 $30.00

3 Listen to the conversation. Circle the correct answer.

June

Danny

1   June is coming to Seattle by train / plane.
2   She's coming in January / February.
3   June and Danny are having lunch / dinner with Mike.
4   They're going to a concert / dance club with Ria.

4 Listen and circle the correct number.

(January) / February 13th / 14th / 15th

June is arriving at 12:20 / 12:30 / 12:40

We're having lunch with Mike at 1:30 / 2:30 / 3:30

We're meeting Ria at 6:15 / 6:50

Speaking 🎧

1 Listen and read.

Let's go to the movies tonight, Gabby.

Sorry, I can't. I'm going to a concert.

That's too bad.

How about going to the movies tonight, Mariella?

I don't think so. I have lots of homework.

That's too bad.

How about going to the movies tonight, Chester?

That's a great idea!

Cool. What movie do you want to see?

2 Look at the Pronunciation box. Listen to the examples.

Now listen and repeat.

3 Listen. Is the phrase accepting or rejecting? Put ✓ for accepting and ✗ for rejecting.

1 _X_   2 ___   3 ___
4 ___   5 ___   6 ___

Listen again and repeat.

4 Practice the dialog with your partner.

5 Change the words in blue. Write a new dialog. Now practice the dialog in class.

Review 11

Vocabulary

1 Write the jobs next to the definitions.

1 give someone a new hair cut _hairstylist_

2 help someone to choose the best clothes to wear _____

3 protect a famous person from, for example, photographers _____

4 teach someone to act better in a film or play _____

5 improve or change the look of someone's face _____

6 help someone to dance well _____

Health problems

2 Match the health problems 1–8 with the solutions A–H.

1 headache   A throat lozenge
2 sprained ankle   B acne cream
3 sore throat   C skin lotion
4 toothache   D aspirin
5 pimple   E hospital
6 sunburn   F tissue
7 blister   G dentist
8 cold   H Band-Aid

Grammar
Present progressive

1 Look at Catalina's diary. Write sentences with *is going to* or *isn't going to*. Some appointments are cancelled.

~~9 a.m. have breakfast with my manager~~

10 a.m. go to the hairstylist's

~~11 a.m. meet my personal trainer at the gym~~

12 p.m. record a new song with Barry

~~give an interview with a magazine~~

2 p.m. open a new art museum

1 _She isn't having breakfast with her manager at 9 a.m._

2 _She is going to the hairstylist's at 10 a.m._

3 _____.

4 _____.

5 _____.

6 _____.

will for offers

2 Write offers for Catalina's problems. Use the verbs below.

call the hairstylist   get you some food
call the dentist   get you an aspirin
change the channel

Catalina: I'm SO hungry!

Assistant: (1) _I'll get you some food_ .

Catalina: I have a terrible headache!

Assistant: (2) _____ .

Catalina: I have a toothache too!

Assistant: (3) _____ .

Catalina: This TV show is SO boring!

Asistant: (4) _____ .

Catalina: I hate my hair color!

Assistant: (5) _____ .

Life experiences

Grammar: present perfect (affirmative / *never*); present perfect (*Have you ever … ?*)
Vocabulary: experiences; embarrassing situations

Vocabulary

1 Match the photos with the words below. Write the correct number next to the words.

5 dye your hair	☐ go parachuting
☐ go on a blind date	☐ have a piercing
☐ go bungee jumping	☐ go skydiving
☐ have a tattoo	☐ go snowboarding

🎧 **Now listen and repeat.**

Recycling

2 Write the activities below in the correct column.

> computer games   judo   rugby   swimming
> karate   skiing   the guitar   surfing

go	play	do
swimming		

Exploring the topic

Reading

1 Read the text. Write the headings in the correct place.

Image change
Going places
Dating
Weird food
Exciting sports

2 🎧 Read and listen to the text. Circle T (True) or F (False).

1 Naomi has had a piercing in her eyebrow.   Ⓣ/ F

2 Luke's hair is blond right now.   T / F

3 Ben has eaten frogs' legs.   T / F

4 Natalia has never eaten insects.   T / F

5 Clive and Vicky have never been parachuting.   T / F

6 Eva has been to the United States.   T / F

7 Clare has never been on a blind date.   T / F

UNUSUAL EXPERIENCES

1 _Image change_

NaOMi I've never had a tattoo, but I have had a piercing once. It's in my eyebrow! My mom hates it, but I think it's cool. Of course, I don't wear it to school!

LUKe I've dyed my hair many times. It's been red, green, blue, blond, and every color in between. Right now my hair is black and short. I kind of like it.

3 _____

VICKY I've done lots of extreme sports. I've been bungee jumping a few times, but I've never been parachuting. I'm going to do that next!

CLive I've never been parachuting – I'm scared of heights! But I've been skiing and snowboarding lots of times.

2 _____

BeN I like trying new foods. I've eaten snails and frogs' legs. I've never eaten insects, but I've accidentally eaten a fly. Uuurgh!

NaTaLia I've eaten insects, on an expedition to the jungle. When you're hungry, anything is tasty!

4 _____

EVa I live in Chile. I've been to an English speaking country, the United States. I've been to New York twice. I've also been to some other countries, for example, Argentina and Ecuador, on an exchange program. Now I'm saving money to go to Africa.

NaO I live in Japan. I've been to London, Paris and Rome, but I've never been to Tokyo, the capital of Japan!

5 _____

CLaRe I've been on a blind date once. Now we're married with three children!

RiK I've never been on a blind date, or any date!

Grammar

Present perfect (affirmative / *never*)

Talking about life experiences

1 Look at the chart.

Affirmative	Never
I / you / we / you / they **have eaten** Chinese food.	I / you / we / you / they **have never been** skiing.
He / She / It **has had** a tattoo.	He / She / It **has never been** to New York.

Take note!

Present perfect

We form the present perfect with *have* / *has* + past participle

Regular participles
Add *-ed*
shout → shouted   play → played

Irregular participles
fall → fallen   have → had   be → been

2 Circle the correct answer.

1. My friend has / have eaten snails.
2. My brother has / have written a song.
3. My parents has / have been to many interesting places in South America.
4. My dad has / have been bungee jumping!
5. My friend and I has / have dyed our hair many times.

3 Write the past participles of the verbs below

Regular	
Verb	Past participle
play	_played_
watch	_____
travel	_____
Irregular	
Verb	Past participle
ride	_____
go	_____
meet	_____

4 Look at the pictures. Fill in the blanks with *have*, *has*, *have never* or *has never*, and the past participles from exercise 3.

Grace

Daniel

Annie

Maria and Pedro

Tom

Julio and Arnoldo

1. Grace _____*has been*_____ parachuting.
2. Daniel _____ a camel.
3. Annie _____ a celebrity.
4. Maria and Pedro _____ by plane.
5. Tom _____ a horror movie.
6. Julio and Arnoldo _____ rugby.

Finished?
Page 111, Puzzle 12A

Over to you!

5 Make sentences about your experiences. Tell the class.

Student A: I have ridden a horse, but I've never ridden a motorcycle.

Student B: I've traveled by train, but I've never traveled by plane.

Building the topic

Embarrassing situations

	Yes, I have.	No, I haven't.
1 Have you ever fallen over in the street?	☐	☐
2 Have you ever talked to the wrong person?	☐	☐
3 Have you ever spilled a drink on somebody?	☐	☐
4 Have you ever fallen asleep in class?	☐	☐
5 Have you ever bumped into a door in a public place?	☐	☐
6 Have you ever snored loudly?	☐	☐
7 Have you ever broken something in a public place?	☐	☐
8 Have you ever worn your shirt inside out?	☐	☐

Vocabulary

1 Match the pictures with the words below. Write the correct letter next to the words.

- *E* bump into
- ☐ wear
- ☐ spill
- ☐ fall asleep
- ☐ fall over
- ☐ break
- ☐ snore
- ☐ talk

🎧 Now listen and repeat.

2 🎧 Read and listen to the questions. Check (✓) *Yes, I have* or *No, I haven't*. Compare your answers in class.

3 Match the verbs 1–7 with the past participles A–G.

1	fall	A	snored
2	wear	B	talked
3	spill	C	bumped
4	break	D	fallen
5	talk	E	spilled
6	bump	F	worn
7	snore	G	broken

Grammar

Present perfect (*Have you ever ... ?*)

Asking about life experiences

1 Look at the chart.

Questions	Short answers
Have I / you / we / you / they **ever snored** loudly?	Yes, I / you / we / you / they **have**. No, I / you / we / you / they **haven't**.
Has he / she / it **ever fallen** over?	Yes, he / she / it **has**. No, he / she / it **hasn't**.

2 Put the words in order to make questions.

1 ever / food on a person / you / spilled / have?

   Have you ever spilled food on a person ?

2 snored / ever / your girlfriend or boyfriend / has / at the movies?

   _____

   _____ ?

3 your friends / broken / in a supermarket / something / ever / have?

   _____

   _____ ?

4 you / in public / have / ever / cried?

   _____

   _____ ?

5 your classmates / in a quiet place / ever / talked loudly / have?

   _____

   _____ ?

6 fallen asleep / your friend / ever / on the bus / has?

   _____

   _____ ?

3 Now write the answers to the questions in exercise 2.

1 *Yes, I have.* or *No, I haven't.*

2 _____

3 _____

4 _____

5 _____

6 _____

4 Look at Jim and Sheila's drawings. Complete the questions and answers.

Jim

Sheila

Sheila

1 *Has Sheila ever been snowboarding* ?

   (go snowboarding) Yes, *she has*.

2 _____ ?

   (eat insects) No, _____ . She has eaten snails.

Jim

3 _____ ?

   (ride a motorbike) Yes, _____ .

4 _____ ?

   (go skiing) No, _____ . He has been surfing

Sheila and Jim

5 _____ ?

   (play the guitar) Yes, _____ .

6 _____ ?

   (play the piano) No, _____ .

Finished?
Page 111, Puzzle 12B

Over to you!

5 Write four *Have you ever ... ?* questions with the verbs from pages 97 and 100. Ask and answer in class.

Student A: Have you ever had a piercing?

Student B: No, I haven't. Have you ever fallen over in the street?

Student A: Yes, I have. Have you ever ... ?

Living English

Review

You need a dice and counters.
Throw the dice.
Answer correctly – stay on the square.
Answer incorrectly – go back two spaces. Wait for your next turn.

Nikki and Ryan are going on vacation – help them get to their destination!

START

1 Name 3 vacation activities.

2 PROBLEM!
Where's Ryan's passport?
Go back to START!

16 Make a correct superlative sentence.

15 PROBLEM!
Nikki and Ryan are lost.
Miss a turn.

14 Ask another player a question about last weekend.
"Did you … last weekend?"

13 Describe the weather yesterday.

17 Complete the sentences.
"At my school, we have to
____. We can't
____."

18 Ask another player a question with the past progressive.
"What … at 7 p.m. last night?"

19 Name 3 natural disasters.

20 Make a correct sentence.
"I was -ing (past progressive), when I (simple past)."

21 PROBLEM!
Nikki and Ryan are arguing.
Go back to START!

4
Complete the sentence.
"In my town there are a lot of ____. There aren't many ____."

Make a correct sentence with "I like / love / hate" and an activity.

5
PROBLEM!
Nikki's skis are broken.
Miss a turn.

Do you speak English?

6

Name 3 household chores.

7

Ask another player "What time do you ... ?"

Describe another player (hair, eyes, clothes).

8

Complete the sentence with the simple past.
"Last year, I _____ on vacation."

12

Name 3 personality adjectives.

11

PROBLEM!
Ryan doesn't understand the language.
Go back 2 spaces.

10

Make a correct comparative sentence.

9

22

23

24

Complete the sentence.
"On vacation, you should ____. You shouldn't ____."

Make a correct sentence.
"On vacation, I'm going to ... ."

Ask another player a question.
"Have you ever ... ?"

FINISH
Well Done!

Review 12

Vocabulary

Experiences

1 Fill in the blanks in the activities below.

1 <u>g</u>o p<u>a</u>ra<u>c</u>hu<u>t</u>i ng
2 _ _ _ _ e a _ _ e _ c i _ _
3 _ _ _ _ n _ _ e _ u _ _ _ n _
4 g_ _ n _ _ _ _ a _ _ i _ g
5 _ a _ _ _ _ t _ _ _
6 _ o _ k _ _ _ _ _ n _
7 _ _ e _ o _ _ _ _ i _
8 _ _ _ n a _ _ _ n _ _ _ _ e

Embarrassing situations

2 Find eight verbs.

fallovert alkwearbumpintofallasleepsnorebreakspill

Grammar

Present perfect (affirmative / *never*)

1 Look at the pictures. Write sentences with the present perfect affirmative (Π) and never (O).

1 He <u>has been</u> to Japan.

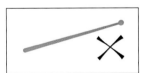
2 We _____ the drums.

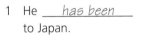
3 She _____ a famous person.

4 They _____ a trophy.

5 I _____ rugby.

6 He _____ a book.

Present perfect (*Have you ever ... ?*)

2 Write the questions with *Have you ever ... ?* and the verbs in parentheses.

1 <u>Have you ever lied</u> to a friend? (lie)
2 _____ your friend's birthday? (celebrate)
3 _____ a nice present? (buy)
4 _____ at your friend? (shout)
5 _____ your friend's boyfriend or girlfriend? (steal)
6 _____ at a bad joke? (laugh)

3 Write your answers to the questions in exercise 2.

1 <u>Yes, I have</u>. or <u>No, I haven't</u>.
2 _____ .
3 _____ .
4 _____ .
5 _____ .
6 _____ .

Reading

1 Answer the questions.

Shaun White is only twenty-one, but he has had many exciting experiences in his short life. He's one of the most successful professional snowboarders in the world, and he's also one of the most talented skateboarders. He has traveled all over the world, and he has competed in the X-Games and the U.S. Open. He has won six gold medals and two silver medals.

1 How old is Shaun White? *He's twenty-one*.
2 Which two sports does he do professionally?
3 Has he traveled all over the world?
4 Which competitions has he competed in?
5 How many gold medals has he won?

engage age

magazine one

puzzle 1a

What does Tom like doing?

y n ~~x~~ r m a o
g ~~x~~ p p e e l
c ~~x~~ m s i u

He likes __ __ __ __ __ __ __ g
__ __ __ __ __ __ __ t __ __ __ a __ __ __ __

puzzle 1b

Do this without using a calculator.

You are driving a bus from London to Edinburgh. In London **17** people get on the bus. In Reading, **6** people get off and **9** people get on. In Oxford, **2** people get off and **4** people get on. In Manchester, **11** people get off and **16** people get on. In York, **3** people get off and **5** people get on. In Newcastle, **6** people get off and **3** people get on. The bus then arrives in Edinburgh.

How many people are on the bus?
What is the name of the bus driver?

puzzle 2a

Do the puzzle. What is Max doing right now?

He **g o e s** to school at 8 o'clock.

He _____ to music in the evening.

He _____ magazines.

_____ movies on the weekend.

He doesn't _____ tennis on the weekend.

He doesn't **d** _____ to school at 8 o'clock.

He _____ **g** _____ in a band.

He doesn't _____ **p** _____ early on the weekend.

puzzle 3a Brain Teaser

Mario is 1.8 meters tall. David is shorter than Mario, but he is taller than Peter. Andy is taller than Mario, but he is shorter than Carl. Tim and Steven are the same height. They are taller than Andy and Carl.

Who is taller than anyone else?
Who is shorter than anyone else?

puzzle 2b What's the chore?

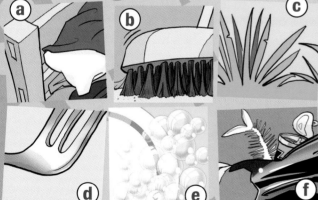

a *make the bed* _____   d _____
b _____   e _____
c _____   f _____

puzzle 3b

Unscramble the words. Use the letters in the boxes to describe Sally.

RATECEVI
☐ ☐ ☐ ☐ ☐ ☐ ☐ ☐

LAETAITVK
☐ ☐ ☐ ☐ ☐ ☐ ☐ ☐ ☐

PTEICTMIVOE
☐ ☐ ☐ ☐ ☐ ☐ ☐ ☐ ☐ ☐ ☐

PEFLULH
☐ ☐ ☐ ☐ ☐ ☐ ☐

S a l l y ____ i s
s ____ ____ ____ ____ b ____ ____

| Back | Stop ✖ | Home 🏠 | Favourites 📄 | History ◯ | Print 📇 |

| Address | | Go |

Washington, USA
Vancouver

| Home | Information | Local Area | Contact us |

3 There are many interesting things to see in Vancouver. Fort Vancouver is older than any other fort on the west coast. There are also many historic houses, beautiful parks and golf courses and very good schools.

1 Vancouver, Washington, USA is a small town. There are about 200,000 people. It is located on the Columbia River, and it is just across the river from Portland, Oregon.

4 Things are changing very fast in our town. They are building new houses all the time. They are also improving the downtownarea of the city, especially on the waterfront. They are opening new restaurants and hotels.

2 People from Vancouver normally work in Portland, because there aren't many jobs in the town. They usually drive to work, so there is a lot of traffic. Many people shop in the bigger city, too, because the prices are lower.

Vancouver has some problems, but it's a great place to live, and it's a fun place to visit too!

1 Read the text above. Which paragraph talks about each of the following?

Things that are happening now _4_
What people normally do __
Attractions __
General information __

2 Think about where you live. Make notes under each of the heading above.

3 Find or take pictures to go with your notes.

4 Design a webpage to introduce your village, town or city.

puzzle 4a

Read the letters following this code: v = s.
Use the code and write the weather words.

A	B	C	D	E	F	G	H	I	J	K	L	M
D	E	F	G	H	I	J	K	L	M	N	O	P
N	O	P	Q	R	S	T	U	V	W	X	Y	Z
Q	R	S	T	U	V	W	X	Y	Z	A	B	C

vxqqb <u>sunny</u>   vqrzb _____   forxgb _____

udlqb _____   zlqgb _____   lfb _____

puzzle 4b

What happened to my family on holiday?
Solve the anagrams.

INK TRUE MY HE   – I <u>HURT</u>   <u>MY</u>   <u>KNEE.</u>

GEL STORM MOB SIT   – MOM _____ _____ .

TALK FED DISC   – DAD _____ _____ .

RIBS LAKE LOG HERE   – LISA _____ _____ _____ .

puzzle 5a

Who played which instrument on the night of the show? Read the clues and write the musicians' names under each instrument.

Rose

- Did Rose play the keyboards? Yes, she did.
- Did Harvey play the guitar? No, he didn't. He hit the instrument with a stick.
- Did Lilia play guitar? No, but she played a similar instrument.
- Did Josh play the keyboards? No, he didn't. But he played an instrument with keys.
- Did Tomas play the guitar that night? Yes, he did.

puzzle 5b

Unscramble the verbs on the disc.
Then complete the biography.

Blink-182 <u>formed</u> the group in San Diego, California.

They _____ their career in 1993.

They _____ the album *Buddha*.

They _____ a contract and sold 4 million copies.

They _____ famous with the album *Dude Ranch*.

DDEERROC

RDSATET

NSEIDG

ACMEBE

FRDEOM

puzzle 6b

What's the message?

| S | A | N | ' | T | H | A | V | E | | F | V | E | | B | E | T | O |

| D | . | | Y | O | U | U | N | ! | Y | O | U | | H | A | | C | A |

| Y | O | U | | | | | | | | | | | | | | | |

| | | | | | | | | | | | | | | | | U | N | ! |

puzzle 6a

Read this funny banner.
Spot the mistakes.

Class 6A win the award for noisiest group, crowdedest and dirtiest classroom, annoyingest students, baddest grammar grades and banner with mowst mistakes.

Franz Ferdinand

1 Read the Franz Ferdinand biography and match the headings to the paragraphs

~~Members~~ **First gig**
First contract
How the band formed
First steps to popularity **Records**

Franz Ferdinand: biography

Members

Alex Kapranos: vocals and guitar. He was born in Gloucestershire, 20 March 1972.

Nicholas McCarthy: guitar, keyboards and vocals. He was born in Blackpool, 13 December 1974.

Bob Hardy: bass. He was born in Bradford, 16 August 1980.

Paul Thomson: drums and vocals. He was born in Edinburgh, 15 September 1977.

Alex wanted to make rock music for people to dance. Drummer Paul and bass guitarist Robert met at Glasgow School of Art. Nick moved from Munich, Germany and met Alex at a party. Nick played the piano and bass guitar, but he decided to be the drummer! And Paul played the guitar.

They formed Franz Ferdinand.

They played their first gig in a Girl Art exhibition in front of 80 people. Many of them watched and most of them danced!

The band decided to move to a bigger place to play music. They rented a place and called it the Chateau. They invited great musicians to the Chateau and played gigs.

The band went to London and met a manager from the Domino Record Company. They signed a contract in 2003.

Franz Ferdinand recorded their first album, *Franz Ferdinand* in 2004. They recorded *You could have it so much better* in 2005.

They had hit records with *Do you want to* and *Walk Away* in 2005.

2 Now choose a band / singer you like. Find their biographical information.

3 Make notes under each of the headings above. You can add news, tours, and albums. Find some photos.

4 Design a fan page and present it to your class.

engage

puzzle 7a

These people were waiting for a bus yesterday.
Label the people with their names.

The person behind Ryan was talking on a cell phone.
The person behind Lucy was eating an ice cream.
The person in front of Adam was reading a newspaper.
The person in front of Yumi was holding an umbrella.

puzzle 7b

Where was Maria at 6 o'clock
last night? Unscramble the letters.

1 Maria wasn't at the <u>bank</u>.
(kbna)
2 She wasn't in her _____.
(taeartpnm)
3 She wasn't in the _____.
(rgaaeg)
4 She wasn't on the _____ _____.
(reif cpeeas)

She was at the _____ _____.
(liecop tosanit)
Maria is a police officer!

puzzle 8a

Read the headlines. Then write the weather
words. What's the mystery word?

| F | L | O | O | D | Water covered city! |

Wind destroyed the whole city!

Wall of water hit beach!

1 meter of snow in 2 hours!

Icy balls hit city!

Ground shook, houses fell!

Flames destroyed forest!

Circular wind!

puzzle 8b

Break the code and write
the sentence.

A	B	C	D	E	F	G	H	I
9				2				

J	J	L	M	N	O	P	Q	R

S	T	U	V	W	X	Y	Z

T O B Y __ A __ __   __ __ E
14 25 18 1   22 24 9 1 11   14 17 2

__ __ __ __ A __   __ __ __ __ __ __ !
15 8 4 14 9 20   24 25 8 13 24 1

puzzle 9a

How many verbs from page 73 can
you make? Which verb is missing?

b s t r i c
e   s   n d
s p m s l
a n t c p d
p i e j u n h
k k s a

puzzle 9b

Use letters from the sentences to
find the two sports. You can only use
the letters once.

I PLAY TWO VERY
COOL SPORTS.
BOTH USE BALLS
AND A NET.

T ☐ ☐ ☐ ☐ ☐
☐ ☐ ☐ ☐ ☐ ☐ ☐ ☐ ☐ ☐

109

1 Read the text and match the headings to the paragraphs.

Recommendation

Equipment

How to play

History

Jai Alai

History

Jai Alai (pronounced high alie) comes from the Basque region of Spain and is over 300 years old. The name means "merry festival" because games often took place during certain festivals. They say that Jai Alai is the fastest game in the world. That is because the ball can go up to 290 km/h.

To play Jai Alai, you need a small, very hard ball and a special basket, a *cesta*. Players wear white pants, a red sash and a colored shirt. They should also wear a helmet to protect the head, because the ball can cause serious injuries. You play the game on a court with three walls.

The rules of Jai Alai are like tennis, racket ball or handball. You can play with two, four or eight players. You throw the ball with your *cesta* and bounce it off the front wall. You win a point when the other team drops or misses the ball.

This sport is amazing to watch and very exciting to play. It's also great exercise because it's so fast. The only problem is that it's very expensive. The equipment is all handmade. A ball costs about $150 and only lasts about 15 minutes! But it's a very cool sport. More people should play it!

2 Now choose an interesting sport. Find information about the history, equipment, rules and where people play it.

3 Make notes under each of the headings above. Find some photos.

4 Write your sports profile. Present it to the class.

puzzle 10a

Unscramble the words. Use the letters in the ⬭ boxes to make the last word.

MBPU ☐⬭☐☐

BCLIM ☐☐☐☐⬭

CHCAT ⬭☐☐☐☐

HRTOW ☐☐☐⬭☐

VIED ☐☐☐⬭

⬭⬭⬭⬭Ⓝ⬭⬭

puzzle 10b

Jake has a lot of problems with his clothes. Unscramble the sentences.

A another this stops or
His pants are too _ _ _ _ _.

Goose hero bias this
His shoes _ _ _ _ _ _ _ _ _.

Unison pigs echo bag hit
His _ _ _ _ _ _ _ _ _ _ enough.

puzzle 11a

Tom, Yao, Tomiko, Marilyn, Ray and Danny are friends. They have five different plans for the evening.

Tom is seeing a movie with his brother.

Yao is playing basketball with her team.

Tomiko is going out for dinner with her mother.

Marilyn is meeting a friend at the mall.

Ray is watching a DVD at home by himself.

What is Danny doing?

puzzle 11b

Kelly has all of these problems. What part of her body doesn't have a problem? Read the clues.

Take the first letter of the first problem, the second letter of the second problem, the seventh letter of the third problem, the fifth letter of the fourth problem, the sixth letter of the fifth problem, and the fourth letter of the sixth problem.

① Ⓣ**OOTHACHE**   ② **COLD**   ③ **HEADACHE**

④ **BLISTER**   ⑤ **SUNBURN**   ⑥ **SPRAINED ANKLE**

Rearrange the letters.

Kelly doesn't have a problem with her _ _ _ _ _ _ _

puzzle 12a   Which photo is Carmen?

A

She has never won a basketball trophy, but she has won a tennis trophy.

B

She has been skiing, but she has never been surfing.

C

She has been to New York, but she has never been to Paris.

puzzle 12b

Are you adventurous? Try our quiz.

Have you ever...

a eaten weird food?   Yes ☐ No ☐
b dyed your hair?   Yes ☐ No ☐
c done an extreme sport?   Yes ☐ No ☐
d been to the jungle or the mountains? Yes ☐ No ☐

3 or 4 Yes: *Wow! You're really adventurous. Be careful!*
1 or 2 Yes: *You are adventurous sometimes. Have fun!*
0 or 1 Yes: *You prefer to stay at home than have adventures. And why not?*

Movie review
Aeon Flux

1 Read the text and match the headings to the paragraphs.

WHERE ~~WHEN~~ **WHO**
RECOMMENDATION **WHAT**

WHEN

400 years in the future.

In a city called Bregna.

Charlize Theron plays Aeon Flux, an assassin. She is a member of the Monicans, a rebel group. John Rafter Lee plays Doctor Goodchild, a scientist and the enemy of Aeon Flux.

A virus killed 99% of the earth's population. The survivors live in a city called Bregna. The city is like a big prison. It's surrounded by walls. A group of scientists rule Bregna. Doctor Goodchild is their powerful leader. Aeon Flux has an important mission. She has to kill Doctor Goodchild and free the city.

This film is exciting with great special effects. Go to see it!

---

2 Now choose a futuristic movie. Here are some ideas: The Island (2005), Robot (2004), The Matrix (2003), Paycheck (2003).

3 Make notes under the headings from the movie review. Find a photo.

4 Write your movie review. Present it to the class.

Grammar summary

Unit 1
Gerunds (-*ing* forms)

like / enjoy / love / don't like / hate + -*ing* form		
I / You / We / They	**love**	sing**ing**.
He / She / It	**enjoys**	read**ing**.

-*ing* form + *be* + adjective		
Running	**is**	awful.
Riding a bike	**is**	fun.

We use gerunds to talk about personal tastes.
Sarah doesn't like running. They love painting.
We use *do/does* + *not* to make gerunds negative.
James and Liz don't like swimming. He doesn't enjoy running.

Spelling rules for -*ing* forms
1 Regular: add -*ing*.
  read – reading
2 One vowel + one consonant: double the consonant + -*ing*.
  run – running
3 Consonant + -*e*: -*e̶/*+ -*ing*.
  ride – riding

much / many / a lot of

Countable	Uncountable
How many people are there?	**How much** noise is there?
There are **a lot of** people.	There's **a lot of** noise.
There are**n't many** people.	There is**n't much** noise.

We use *much / many / a lot of* to talk about quantity.
How many oranges are there? There are a lot of oranges. There isn't much milk.
We use *many* with countable nouns.
There aren't many DVDs in the library.
We use *much* with uncountable nouns.
There isn't much snow.
We use *a lot of* with countable and uncountable nouns.
There are a lot of students.
We form questions with *How* + *much / many*.
How much money is there?

Unit 2
Simple present and present progressive

Simple present	Present progressive
I watch TV **every evening**.	He's watching a soccer match **right now**.
She doesn't play tennis **on the weekend**.	They aren't playing basketball **right now**.
Do they have dinner **at six o'clock**?	Are you eating a burger **right now**?
When do you get up?	What is he doing **right now**?

We use the simple present to talk about regular activities.
I play a lot of sport. They travel to Patagonia every summer.
We use the present progressive to talk about things that are happening right now.
Maria's speaking on her cell phone right now. We aren't winning the tennis game right now.

have to

Obligation		No obligation	
I / You	**have to** set the table.	I / You	**don't have to** wash the dishes.
He / She / It	**has to** cut the grass.	He / She / It	**doesn't have to** make lunch.
You / We / They	**have to** wash the dishes.	You / We / They	**don't have to** set the table.

Questions	Short answers
Do you **have to** help in the house?	Yes, I do. / No, I don't.
Does he / she **have to** help in the house?	Yes, she does. / No, she doesn't.

We use *have to* to talk about obligations.
I have to do my homework. Sarah has to clean her room.
We use *don't have to* to talk about absence of obligation.
He doesn't have to wear a school uniform. They don't have to take the English test.

Grammar summary

Unit 3
Short comparative adjectives

adjective + -er + than				
Mario	is	short**er**	**than**	Damon.
Mario's jeans	are	loos**er**	**than**	Damon's jeans.

We use comparatives to talk about differences between two things or people.
Alex's hair is curlier than James's.
Their car is bigger than our car.
Short adjectives form short comparatives:
My hair is shorter than Caroline's hair.
Her cellphone is newer than Liz's phone.

Spelling rules for short comparative adjectives

Regular:
1 add -er or -r
   tall → taller
   long → longer
   loose → looser
2 *y* + -ier
   curly → curlier
   wavy → wavier

3 double consonant + -er
   big → bigger
   Irregular:
   good → better
   bad → worse

Long comparative adjectives

more + adjective + than					
Mario	is	**more**	helpful	**than**	Damon.
Jan and Kim	are	**more**	sociable	**than**	Karen.

We use long comparatives to compare people and things with long adjectives.
Math is more difficult than History.
We form long comparatives with *more* + adjective + *than*.
Michelle is more beautiful than Tara.

Unit 4
was / were

Affirmative	Negative
I / He / She / It **was** in Brazil last year.	I / He / She / It **wasn't** in Laos last year.
You / We / You / They **were** in Brazil last year.	You / We / They **weren't** in Laos last year.
There **was** a big temple.	There **wasn't** any snow.
There **were** mountains.	There **weren't** many tourists.

We use simple past *be* (*was / were*) to talk about something in the past.
Jamie was in a museum. Kate and Anna were friends.
We use *not* to make *was / were* negative.
She wasn't happy. We weren't in California.
We form *yes / no* questions with *was / were* + subject.
Were they on the beach? Yes, they were.

Simple past (affirmative)

Regular	Irregular
I / You / He / She It faint**ed**.	I / You / He / She / It **felt** sick.
You / We / They slipp**ed**.	You / We / They **got** blisters.

We use the simple past to talk about the past.
I walked to the movie theater.
He found a dollar.

Regular verbs end in -ed.
We liked the movie. She tried to win.
They planned a party.

Irregular verbs change completely.
Amy took a cookie. My dad called the school.

Unit 5
Simple past (*yes / no* questions)

Questions	Short answers
Did I / you / he / she / it buy a record yesterday?	Yes, I / you / he / she / it **did**. / No, I / you / he / she / it **didn't**.
Did we / you / they play soul music?	Yes, we / you / they **did**. / No, we / you / they **didn't**.

Negative
I / You / He / She / It **didn't win** an award in 1994.
We / You / They **didn't play** hip hop.

We use simple past questions to ask about the past.
Did they understand the class?
Did he win the game?
Form *yes / no* questions with *did* + subject + infinitive.
Did she drive the car?
Did Sam take the hamburger?
Form the simple past negative with subject + *didn't* + infinitive.
No, she didn't drive the car.
No, he didn't take the hamburger.

Simple past (*wh-* questions)

wh- questions
What did you do last night?
Where did he go on vacation?
When did she record an album?
Why did they win an award?
How did you start your career?
How many records did they sell?

Form simple past wh- questions with *wh-* question word + *did* + subject + infinitive.
Where did Mia buy her skirt?
When did they do their project?

Unit 6

Superlative adjectives

the + superlative + noun
Taipei 101 is **the tallest** building in the world.
Manila is **the most crowded** city in the world.

We use superlatives to talk about unique things.

It is the best painting in the class. The Pacific Ocean is the biggest ocean in the world.

Spelling rules for superlative adjectives

Short adjectives	Long adjectives
1 add *-est* or *-st*	interesting ➔ the most
tall ➔ the tallest	interesting
large ➔ largest	
2 -*y* + *-iest*	**Irregular**
crazy ➔ the craziest	good ➔ the best
3 double consonant + *-iest*	bad ➔ the worst
big ➔ the biggest	

have to / can't

Necessary	Forbidden
You **have to** carry your passport.	You **can't** camp outdoors.
You **have to** buy a ticket.	You **can't** drop litter.

We use *have to* to talk about things that are necessary.
You have to go to school.

We use *can't* to talk about things that are forbidden.
You can't talk on your cell phone in class.

don't have to / can

Not necessary	Possible
You **don't have to** go on an organized tour.	You **can** sleep in the guard towers.
We **don't have to** wear a school uniform.	We **can** wear what we want to school.

We use *don't have to* to talk about things that are not necessary.
We don't have to go home early.

We use *can* to talk about things that are possible.
We can stay out late.

Unit 7

Past progressive (affirmative / negative)

Affirmative	Negative
I **was** arguing.	I **wasn't** fighting.
You **were** running.	You **weren't** walking.
He / She / It **was** hiding.	He / She / It **wasn't** shouting.
We / You / They **were** talking.	We / You / They **weren't** hiding.

We use the past progressive to talk about actions in progress in the past.
I was talking to Miranda in the park.
They weren't playing soccer on Saturday.

We form the past progressive negative with subject + *was / were + not* + verb *-ing* form.
He wasn't reading the newspaper.
Melissa and Jen weren't playing chess.

Past progressive (questions)

yes / no questions	Answers
Was I runn**ing**?	Yes, I **was**. / No, I **wasn't**.
Were you hid**ing**?	Yes, you **were**. / No, you **weren't**.
Was he / she / it argu**ing**?	Yes, he / she / it **was**. No, he / she / it **wasn't**.
Were we / you / they fight**ing**?	Yes, we / you / they **were**. No, we / you / they **weren't**.

wh- questions	
Where were you go**ing**?	I was going to the movies.
What were you do**ing** at 9 p.m.?	I was doing my homework.

We use the past progressive to ask about actions in progress in the past.
Was Catherine singing? What were Rosie and Emily listening to?
Form *yes / no* questions with *Was / Were* + subject + verb *-ing* form.
Was he eating? Yes, he was.
Were you writing a letter? No, I wasn't.

Form *wh-* questions with *wh-* question + *was / were* + subject + verb *–ing* form.
Where were you swimming? I was swimming at the swimming pool.
Why was Scott waiting? Scott was waiting for the bus.

Unit 8
Past progressive and simple past

Action in progress	Completed action
He **was studying** climate change.	A tornado **hit** New York.
They **weren't having** dinner.	We **didn't go** out last night.

We use the past progressive to talk about actions in progress in the past.
She was playing volleyball.
They were talking in the kitchen.
We use the simple past to talk about completed actions in the past.
I made a cake. J.K. Rowling wrote Harry Potter and the Sorcerer's Stone.

Adverbs of manner

Regular adverbs		
Adjective	Adverb	Example
quiet	quiet**ly**	She was talking **quietly**.
happy	happ**ily**	The girl was smiling **happily**.
easy	eas**ily**	He passed the exam **easily**.
Irregular adverbs		
good	**well**	She plays tennis **well**.
hard	**hard**	She was working **hard**.
fast	**fast**	She ran **fast**.

We use adverbs of manner to talk about how we do things.
She walks slowly. They read the text carefully.
We form most regular adverbs by adding *-ly* to the adjective.
The team played badly.

If an adjective ends with *-y*, the adverb ends with *-ily*.
Emily sang happily.
Some adverbs are irregular and don't end with *-ly*.
He plays the guitar well.

Unit 9
should / shouldn't

Affirmative	Negative
You **should** warm up.	You **shouldn't** wear long shorts.
Questions	**Answers**
Should I exercise more?	Yes, you **should**. / No, you **shouldn't**.
What **should** I do?	You **should** have a lesson.

We use *should / shouldn't* to give advice.
You should buy that t-shirt.
You shouldn't sit in the sun all day.
We use *should* with an infinitive.
You should go home.
The form of *should* is the same for all persons.
I should go home. He should go home.
They should go home.
We use the question form *should I / we* + verb to ask for advice.
Should I wear a coat? What should I wear?

going to

Affirmative	Negative
We're **going to** play tennis.	We aren't **going to** do karate.
She's **going to** go horse riding.	She isn't **going to** go cycling.
Questions	**Answers**
Are we **going to** exercise every day?	Yes, we **are**. / No. we **aren't**.
What are you **going to** do?	I'm **going to** play lacrosse.

We use *going to* to talk about plans and resolutions.
I am going to pass the test.
She is going to eat more fruit.
We form *going to* sentences with subject + *be* + *going to* + infinitive.
Matt is going to make a movie.
They aren't going to visit David.
Form *yes / no* questions with *be* + subject + *going to* + infinitive.
Is she going to leave?

Unit 10

will / won't

Affirmative	Negative
I / You / He / She / It **will** travel to space.	I / You / He / She / It **won't** play zero gravity sports.
We / You / They **will** float in space.	We / You / They **won't** travel to space.
There will be zero gravity sports.	There **won't be** cars.

We use *will / won't* to make predictions about the future.
I will go to Australia. There won't be any cars.
We make *will / won't* sentences with subject + *will / won't* + infinitive.
Dan won't be here next week.
They won't come to my house.

too / not enough

too + adjective	not + adjective + enough
It's **too** dangerous.	It is**n't** close **enough**.

We form *too* sentences with *too* + adjective.
The shoes are too big.
We form *not enough* sentences with *not* + adjective + *enough*.
The jacket is not big enough.

Unit 11

Present progressive

Affirmative	Negative
I**'m having** lunch with Carol at twelve thirty.	I**'m not playing** tennis tomorrow.

Questions	Answers
Are you **meeting** Maria at eight o'clock?	Yes, I **am**. / No, I**'m not**.
What time **are** you **going** to the movies?	At eight o'clock.

We use time expressions with the present progressive to talk about future arrangements.
They're going to the movie theater at seven-thirty.
She's running a marathon this afternoon.

will (offers)

Problem	Offer
I have a headache.	**I'll get** you some aspirin.
I'm hungry.	**I'll make** you a sandwich.

We use *will* to make offers.
I'll carry your suitcase. We'll make you a cake.

Unit 12

Present perfect (affirmative / never)

Affirmative	Never
I / you / we / you / they **have eaten** Chinese food.	I / you / we / you / they **have never been** skiiing.
He / She / It **has gotten** a tattoo.	He / She / It **has never been** to New York.

We use the present perfect to talk about life experiences.
She has eaten in expensive restaurants.
We form the present perfect with subject + *have / has* + past participle.
I have traveled to India. They have seen the Taj Mahal.
Use *never* to form negative sentences about life experiences.
Jake has never visited a museum.

Regular and irregular participles
Some participles are regular.
Add *-ed*
shout ➜ shouted, play ➜ played
Some participles are irregular.
fall ➜ fallen   have ➜ had   be ➜ been

Present perfect (*Have you ever*)

Questions	Short answers
Have I / you / we / you / they **ever snored** loudly?	Yes, I / you / we / you / they **have**. No, I / you / we / you / they **haven't**.
Has he / she / it **ever fallen** over?	Yes, he / she / it **has**. No, he / she / it **hasn't**.

We use present perfect questions to ask about life experiences.
Have you seen King Kong?
Has he bought an iPod?
Form present perfect questions with *have / has* + subject + *ever* + past participle.
Have you ever walked up a mountain?
Has Kelly ever met your mom?

Word list

Remember

Feelings
angry /'æŋgri/
happy /'hæpi/
nervous /'nərvəs/
scared /skerd/
surprised /sər'praızd/
tired /taiərd/

Food
apples /'æplz/
cheese /tʃiz/
chicken /'tʃɪkən/
milk /mɪlk/
muffins /'mʌfənz/
soda /'soudə/
yogurts /'yougərts/

Clothes
boots /butz/
cap /kæp/
gloves /glʌvz/
hat /hæt/
jacket /'dzækɪt/
jersey /'dʒərzi/
shorts /ʃorts/
sneakers /'snikərz/
sunglasses /sənglæsiz/
T-shirt /'tiʃərt/

Parts of the body
body /'badi/
eyes /aɪz/
feet /fit/
hands /hændz/
head /hɛd/

Adjectives (objects)
big /bɪg/
cheap /tʃip/
expensive /ɪk'spenslv/
hard /hard/
heavy //hɛvi/
light /laɪt/
long /lɔŋ/
new /nu/
old /ould/
short /ʃaut/
small /smɔl/
soft /sɔft/
thick /θɪk/
thin /θin/

Appearance
blond /bland/
curly /kərli/
straight /streit/
tall /tɔl/
wavy /weivi/

Unit 1

Sports and hobbies
acting /'æktɪŋ/
painting /peintɪŋ/
playing in a band /'pleiɪŋ ɪn ə bænd/
playing soccer /'pleiɪŋ 'sakər/
running /'rənɪŋ/
scuba diving /'daivɪŋ/
shopping /'ʃapɪŋ/
working on a computer /'wərkɪŋ an ə kəm'pyutər/

City life
tall buildings /tɔl 'bɪldɪŋz/
entertainment /ˌentər'teinmənt/
litter /'lɪtər/
noise /nɔiz/
open spaces /'oupən 'speisiz/
pollution /pə'luʃən/
houses /'hausiz/
traffic /'træfɪk/

Living English
balcony /'bælkəni/
population /papy'əleiʃn/

Review 1
charity /'tʃærəti/

Unit 2

Activities
eat fast food /it fæst fud/
go climbing /gou 'klaimɪŋ/
go to school /gou tə skul/
listen to music /'lɪsən tə 'myuzɪk/
play an instrument /plei ən 'ɪnstrəmənt/
play basketball /plei 'bæskɪt bɔl/
read magazines /ˌmægə'zin, 'mægəˌzin/
watch movies /watʃ 'muviz/

Household chores
clean (your) room /klin (yʊr) rum, rʊm/
cut the grass /kət ðe græs/
make (your) bed /meik (yʊr) bed/
make lunch /meik ləntʃ/
put away /pʊt ə'wei/
set the table /set ðə 'teibəl/
take out the garbage /teik aut ðə 'garbɪdʒ/
wash the dishes /woʃ, waʃ ðə dɪʃiz/

Living English
diaper /'daɪpər/
dust /dʌst/
judge /dʒʌdʒ/
odor /'oudər/
venom /'vɛnəm/

Other
glacier /'gleiʃər/
pancake /'pænkeɪk/

Review 2
makeup /'meikʌp/
potion /'pouʃn/

Unit 3

Physical appearance
curly /kərli/
long /lɔŋ/
loose /lus/
short /ʃaut/
straight /streit/
tall /tɔl/
tight /tait/
wavy /weivi/
low /lou/
high /haɪ/

Personality
competitive /kəm'petətɪv/
creative /kri'eitɪv/
disorganized /dɪ'sərgənaizd/
helpful /'helpfəl/
talkative /'tɔkətɪv/
sociable /'souʃəbl/

Living English
action hero /'ækʃn 'hɪrou/
fairy tale character /'fɛri teɪl 'kærəktər/
alien /'eiliən/
grunge /grʌnʒ/

Magazine 1
downtown /daʊn'taʊn/
get off /gɛt ɔf/
get on /gɛt ɔn/
golf course /galf kɔrs/
waterfront /'wɔtərfrʌnt/

Unit 4

Weather
cloudy /'klaudi/
cold /kould/
hot /hat/
icy /'aisi/
rainy /'reini/
snowy /'snoui/
sunny /'səni/
warm /wɔrm/
windy /'windi/

Vacation problems
faint /feint/
feel sick /'fiəl/ /sɪk/
get blisters /get 'blɪstərz/
hurt /hərt/
slip /slip/
sprain /sprein/

Living English
adrenaline /ə'drɛnlɪn/
injury /'ɪndʒəri/
pain /peɪn/
reflex /'riflɛks/

Review 4
shark /ʃark/

Unit 5

Musical instruments
bass /'bæs/
drums /drəms/
guitar /gɪ'tar/
keyboard /kibɔrd/
microphone /'maikrəˌfoun/
piano /pɪ'ænou/

Biography verbs
become famous /bɪ'kʌm 'feiməs/
grow up /grou əp/
have a hit record /hæv ə hɪt 'rekərd/
record an album /rɪ'kɔrd ən 'ælbəm/
sign a contract /sain ə kə'trækt/
start her career /start hər kə'rɪr/
was born /wəz bɔrn/
win an award /wɪn ən ə'wɔrd/

Living English
form /fɔrm/
member /'mɛmbərz/
package /'pækɪdʒ/
virtual /'vərtʃuəl/

Review 5
appear /ə'pɪr/

Unit 6

Describing a place
crowded /kraudəd/
deep /dip/
large /lardʒ/
long /lɔŋ/
narrow /'nærou/
small /smɔl/
tall /tɔl/
wide /waid/

Travel activities
bargain /'bargən/
buy a ticket /bai ə 'tɪkɪt/
camp /kæmp/
carry your passport /'kæri yɔr 'pæs,pɔrt/
drop litter /drap 'lɪtər/
follow the rules /'falou ðə rulz/
take a tour /teik ə tʊr/
use a credit card /yus ə 'krɛdɪt kard/

Other
staircase /'stɛrkeɪs/

Review 6
historical monuments /hɪ'stɔrɪkl 'manyəmənts/
nightlife /'naɪtlaɪf/

Unit 7

Conflict verbs
argue /'ar,gyu/
fight /fait/
hide /haid/
hit /hɪt/
shout /ʃaut/

Places
apartment /ə'partmənt/
bank /bæŋk/
fire escape /'faiər ɪ'skeip/
garage /gə'raʒ/
police station /pə'lis 'steiʃən/
street corner /strit 'kɔrnər/

Living English
burglar /'bərglər/
convenience store /kən'vinyəns stɔr/
dummy /'dʌmi/
freeway /'friwei/
gas station /gæs 'steiʃn/

Other
gun /gʌn/
knife /na ɪf/
sidewalk /'saɪdwɔk/
witness /'wɪtnəs/
wrecked /'rekt/

Unit 8

Natural disasters
blizzard /'blɪzərd/
earthquake /'ərθ,kweik/
flood /flʌd/
forest fire /'fɔrɪst, 'farɪst 'faiər/
hailstorm /'heiəlstɔrm/
hurricane /'hərə,kein/
tornado /tər'neidou/
tsunami /su'nærmi/

Adverbs of manner
angrily /'æŋgrili/
carefully /'kerfəli/
happily /'hæpili/
hard /hard/
loudly /laudli/
quickly /'kwɪkli/
quietly /'kwaiɪtli/
well /wel/

Living English
crawl /krɔl/
rope /roup/

Review 8
hunter /'hʌntər/
survivor /sər'vaivər/
wing /wɪŋ/

Unit 9

Exercise verbs
bend /bend/
hit /hɪt/
jump /dʒəmp/
kick /kɪk/
land /lænd/
pass /pæs/
spin /spin/
stretch /stretʃ/

Sports
do karate /du kə'rati/
do track /du træk/
go cycling /du 'saiklɪŋ/

go horseback riding /gou 'hɔrsbæk 'raidɪŋ/
go water-skiing /gou 'wɔtər skiɪŋ/
play basketball /plei 'bæskit,bɔl/
play golf /plei galf, gɔlf/
play lacrosse /plei lə'krɔs/

Living English
kung fu /kʌŋ fu/

Magazine 3
fence /fɛns/
sash /sæʃ/

Unit 10

Actions
bounce /'bauns/
bump into /bəmp 'ɪntə/
catch /kætʃ/
climb /klaim/
dive /daiv/
drop /drap/
float /flout/
throw /θrou/

Describing places
close /klous/
cold /kould/
dangerous /'deindʒ(ə)rəs/
dry /drai/
far /far/
safe /seif/
stable /'steibəl/
unstable /,ən'steibəl/
warm /wɔrm/
wet /wet/

Living English
evaporate /ɪ'væpəreit/
freeze /friz/
fry /frai/
polar bear /'poulər bɛr/
species /'spiʃiz/

Other
gravity /'grævəti/
orbit /'ɔrbət/
tourism /'tʊrɪzəm/

Review 10
harmony /'harməni/

Unit 11

TV jobs
acting coach /'æktɪŋ koutʃ/
bodyguard /'badigard/
dance teacher /dæns titʃər/
hairstylist /her'stailɪst/
makeup artist /'meik,əp 'artist/
stylist /'stailɪst/

Health problems
cold /kould/
headache /hedeik/
pimple /'pɪmpəl/
sore finger /sɔr 'fɪŋgər/
sore throat /sɔr θrout/
sprained ankle /spreind 'æŋkəl/
sunburn /sənbərn/
toothache /tuθeik/

Living English
acupuncture /'ækyəpʌŋktʃər/
massage /mə'saʒ/

Other
audition /ɔ'dɪʃn/
contestant /kən'tɛstənt/

Unit 12

Experiences
go bungee jumping /gou 'bəndʒi dʒəmpɪŋ/
dye your hair /dai yɔr her/
have a piercing /hæv ə pɪrsɪŋ/
have a tattoo /hæv ə tæ'tu/
go on a blind date /gou an ə blaind deit/
go parachuting /gou 'pærə,ʃutɪŋ/
go skydiving /gou 'skaidaivɪŋ/
go snowboarding /gou snoubɔrdɪŋ/

Embarrassing situations
break /breik/
bump into /bəmp 'ɪntə/
fall asleep /fɔl ə'slip/
fall over /fɔl 'ouvər/
snore /snɔr/
spill /spɪl/
talk /tɔk/
wear /wer/

Other

eyebrow /ˈaɪbraʊ/
frog /frɒg/
insect /ˈnsɛkt/
snail /sneɪl/

Review 12

trophy /ˈtroʊfi/

Magazine 4

assassin /əˈsæsn/
rebel /ˈrɛbl/
revolutionary /rɛvəˈluʃnɛri/
virus /ˈvaɪrəs/

Verb list

Irregular verbs

babysit	babysat	babysat	hurt	hurt	hurt
be	was/were	been	know	knew	known
become	became	become	make	made	made
begin	began	begun	meet	met	met
break	broke	broken	put	put	put
build	built	built	read	read	read
buy	bought	bought	ride	rode	ridden
catch	caught	caught	run	ran	run
come	came	come	see	saw	seen
cut	cut	cut	sell	sold	sold
do	did	done	send	sent	sent
draw	drew	drawn	set	set	set
drink	drank	drunk	sing	sang	sung
drive	drove	driven	sink	sank	sunk
eat	ate	eaten	sit	sat	sat
fall	fell	fallen	sleep	slept	slept
feel	felt	felt	speak	spoke	spoken
fight	fought	fought	steal	stole	stolen
find	found	found	swim	swam	swum
fly	flew	flown	take	took	taken
get	got	gotten	tell	told	told
give	gave	given	think	thought	thought
go	went	been (gone)	throw	threw	thrown
grow	grew	grown	wear	wore	worn
have	has/have	had	win	won	won
hide	hid	hidden	write	wrote	written
hit	hit	hit			